UNITED *in* JESUS

UNITED *in* JOY

Sermons on Philippians

Edited by

RAY VAN NESTE & JUSTIN WAINSCOTT

UNION UNIVERSITY | **PRESS**

Ray Van Neste
1050 Union University Drive
Jackson, TN 38305

Published by Union University Press
978-1-964086-02-6

CONTENTS

ACKNOWLEDGEMENTS

There are several people without whom this book never could have come into being. First of all, we are grateful for the preachers who participated in this series, and we thank them for their willingness to help take their chapel sermons and prepare them for publication in this book. Mr. Jeff Thompson once again created the cover design and formatted the book. Mrs. Karen Jones helped with the audio transcriptions and in tracking down all the necessary details. We are grateful to both of them for their time and effort.

We appreciate all the faculty, staff, and students at Union University, and we are grateful to be a part of this community which regularly gathers for chapel. We particularly want to thank our president, Dr. Dub Oliver, and our provost, Dr. Jacob Shatzer. Their hearty support of chapel and its importance to our work here at Union shapes a culture that values our gathered worship from which this project emerges.

Finally, we want to thank our wives, Tammie (Ray) and Anna (Justin), for their ongoing love and support.

CONTRIBUTORS

Brian Arnold serves as Senior Pastor of First Baptist Church in Paducah, Kentucky.

Andy Davis serves as Senior Pastor of First Baptist Church in Durham, North Carolina.

Ken Lewis serves as Dean of the Memphis College of Urban and Theological Studies (MCUTS) at Union University and Senior Pastor of Briarwood Church in Memphis, Tennessee.

Phil Newton serves as Director of Pastoral Care and Mentoring for the Pillar Network.

Justin Perry serves as Lead Pastor of Covenant Life Church in Tampa, Florida.

Ray Van Neste serves as Vice President for University Ministries and Dean of the School of Theology and Missions at Union University.

Justin Wainscott serves as Associate Dean for University Ministries and of the School of Theology and Missions at Union University.

Hershael York serves as Dean of the School of Theology and Victor and Louise Lester Professor of Christian Preaching at The Southern Baptist Theological Seminary in Louisville, Kentucky.

PREFACE

Chapel is an important part of our life together at Union University, giving us an opportunity to gather twice a week as a community to hear from God in his Word and respond to him. These services remind us of our grounding in Scripture and of the centrality of Jesus Christ to our lives. For the last several years in the Spring semester we have dedicated certain chapel services to sermons working their way through a specific book of the Bible. In the Spring of 2024, we focused on Philippians. Our community has been blessed by these series over the years, so we thought there would be value in gathering this most recent series into written form for wider dissemination.

Philippians is commonly listed among people's favorite books of the Bible. Dr. Paul Caudill wrote, "The book of Philippians is one of the loveliest portions of the Bible."[1] Indeed Dr. A. T. Robertson, that giant of New Testament scholarship, said, "Nowhere does Paul have more 'charm,' to use Ramsay's phrase, than in Philippians. Nowhere is he more vital and more powerful. Paul was not merely a man of supreme genius and high culture but one who let himself go completely in spiritual abandonment to the love and life of Jesus."[2] It has been our pleasure to work through this letter together.

Two of the most consistent and significant themes in Philippians (and in these sermons) are unity and joy, both of which are clearly

---

[1] R. Paul Caudill. *Philippians: A Translation with Notes* (Blue Ridge Press of Boone, Inc., 1980), 9.

[2] A. T. Robertson, *Paul's Joy in Christ: Studies in Philippians* (Revised and edited by W.C. Strickland) (Broadman Press, nd), v.

grounded in Jesus Christ. Therefore, our title for this book—*United in Jesus, United in Joy*—arises from that reality.

In preparing these sermons for publication, we have not sought to turn them into essays but have intentionally maintained the oral, sermonic form in all their particularity.

Our hope is that this work might encourage other Christians as they learn more about this particular book of the Bible, the truths it proclaims, and the Savior it exalts. We also hope it will be a resource for other preachers as they prepare to preach through Philippians.

Ray Van Neste and Justin Wainscott

Chapter 1

THE PRAYER LIFE
OF THE APOSTLE PAUL

Philippians 1:1-11

Andy Davis[1]

Introduction

I'd like to ask that you turn in your Bibles to Philippians chapter 1. We're going to look at the beginning of this great epistle that Paul wrote to the Philippians, and we're going to look at Paul's prayer—his model prayer—for the Philippians. And as I as a Christian think about prayer, as I try to understand it, my mind goes to the final book of the Bible, Revelation. And in that vision that the apostle John had on the island of Patmos, he had a vision of a doorway standing open in heaven, and he was invited supernaturally to move through that doorway into the presence of God, into the heavenly realms. And he saw immediately the central reality of the universe, which is a throne with someone seated on it.

God enthroned is the central reality of the universe. And that's what's unveiled in the book of Revelation: the sovereign God, the King of the universe, and in concentric circles around him twenty-four elders and living creatures and a hundred million angels ready to do his bidding, and a throne at the center of everything. And then at the end of that book—indeed, at the end of the Bible (Revelation 22)—we have that same throne. And Almighty God is seated on that throne, and a river of the water of life is flowing from that throne, clear as crystal down the center of the New Jerusalem.

[1] Andy Davis is Senior Pastor of First Baptist Church, Durham, North Carolina.

And so that concept of Almighty God enthroned, and everything coming from that throne, is what prayer is all about. As Paul says in his doxology in Romans 11, "For from him and through him and to him are all things" (Rom 11:36). Or as James says, "Every good and perfect gift is from above" (James 1:17). Or again, as Psalm 145 says, "He opens his hand and satisfies the desire of every living creature" (Psalm 145:16). Every good thing you could ever want, both in the spiritual realm and in the physical, starts in the hand of God. And God wants us to know that. And he wants us to come to him and ask him for it, so that he would open his hand and give you the desires of your heart. We are far too independent. And salvation, in part, is teaching us how absolutely dependent we are on God—"for in him we live and move and have our being" (Acts 17:28). Everything comes from God, and prayer is part of us learning that.

And so, we go to Philippians to try to learn how to pray. And we need this help, because Romans 8:26 says very plainly, "The Spirit helps us in our weakness." We do not know what to pray for. And not only do we not know what to pray for, we don't know how to pray. And so, the Holy Spirit has been given to help us with prayer (among other things). And he teaches us what we ought to pray for. And he does that powerfully and primarily in Scripture, and I would say especially in the epistles. As you look at how Paul prays for the Philippians, we get educated on how we ought to pray.

Now, we need to understand something about prayer. Prayer is in no way reshaping the mind of God. We're not giving God any new ideas. We're not giving God any better ways of doing things. Neither are we trying to wear him down and persuade him to do something in a way he hadn't planned on doing. It's none of those things. Rather, prayer is us getting on God's agenda, getting on God's timetable, and pleading with him to do the things he's already decided to do but just hasn't done yet. That's what prayer is.

And so, the Holy Spirit gives us assistance in Philippians 1:1-11 to teach us how we ought to pray, what we ought to pray for. And that's what we're going to do in the brief time we have together.

Context

Let's look at some context. Paul is writing to a Philippian church that he dearly loves. He's very affectionate toward this church. You remember how the church was planted. The story is told in Acts 16, how Paul and his entourage were just not really sure where to go next. They were blocked in every direction. And then Paul has a vision of a man from Macedonia saying, "Come over and help us" (Acts 16:9). And Paul and his team, including Silas, concluded that God was calling them westward toward Europe to preach the gospel there. And so, he goes over there, and in the course of time plants a church.

And it begins with a woman, a wealthy woman named Lydia—a dealer in purple cloth who comes to faith and then invites Paul and Silas and the team to stay with her at her mansion. It begins there, and then there's an incredible story in Acts 16 of how Paul and Silas were arrested and publicly beaten and thrown in jail and their feet were put in the stocks. And it's dark and their backs are bleeding and they're hungry. And what are they doing at midnight but singing praise songs to Jesus? And all the other prisoners are listening. And then suddenly God sent a miraculous, surgical-strike earthquake that caused their chains to fall off and the prison doors to fly open, but no prisoner escaped. And the Philippian jailer runs out in the middle of the night and is about to fall on his sword—commit suicide—because as a Roman jailer, he would have been responsible for escaped prisoners. But they're all there. Paul calls out from the darkness and says, "Do not harm yourself. We're all here." And the jailer goes in and gets Paul and Silas, brings them out, falls trembling before them, and says, "What must I do to be saved?"

What a great question. And they preached the gospel, and that night the Philippian jailer and his family heard the gospel, they repented, they believed, and they became Christians. This is the beginning of the Philippian church.

Paul, however, as a traveling evangelist, moving around from place to place, left Philippi and went on to other works. And in the course of time, the Philippian Church that he had helped plant, along with Silas and his team, heard that Paul was in prison again and that he needed support. And so, they sent money by a man named Epaphroditus.

And so, really, Philippians is the greatest thank you letter in history. When you receive a gift, you should write a thank you note. So, that's what it is, among other things. So, he's thanking them for their partnership in the gospel financially. And he begins by writing to the Philippian church and its leaders.

Look at verses 1-2: "Paul and Timothy, servants of Christ Jesus, to all the saints in Christ Jesus of Philippi, together with the overseers and deacons: Grace and peace to you from God our Father and the Lord Jesus Christ." So, Paul expresses his affection and his love for them. He thanks them for the money that they had sent for his support. But he also instructs them; he's going to teach them. And among the things that he wants to teach them is how he prays for them. And in teaching them, he's teaching us. So, the Holy Spirit wants us to learn from these verses how we ought to pray and what we ought to pray for.

So, we're going to walk through these verses—verses 3 through 11—to see first the character of Paul's prayer life (what he's like, what his heart is like in prayer). And then secondly, the content of Paul's prayer life (some of the content—not everything, but just what he's praying for in these verses). And then thirdly, the ultimate goal of Paul's prayer life. So, those are the three aspects of what we're going to do as we walk through this passage.

So, let's begin with the character of Paul's prayer life in verses 3-8.

1. The character of Paul's prayer life (1:3-8)

"I thank my God every time I remember you. In all my prayers for all of you, I always pray with joy because of your partnership in the gospel from the first day until now. Being confident of this, that he who began a good work in you will carry it on to completion until the day of Christ Jesus. It is right for me to feel this way about all of you, since I have you in my heart. For whether I am in chains or defending and confirming the gospel, all of you share in God's grace with me. God can testify how I long for all of you with the affection of Christ Jesus" (1:3-8).

So, the character of how Paul prays—the nature of his relationship with them—flows in these verses. It starts with thankfulness. Paul expresses thankfulness to God in his prayers for them.

He's deeply thankful to God for their faith, their conversion, for their being Christians at all, and for their friendship and their partnership in the gospel ministry. He gives God the credit for all of that. From that throne of Almighty God flowed all of these blessings. He thanks God for their conversion because he considers God responsible for it. So, thankfulness.

And then, remembrance. Paul thinks about his relationship with them—it's what makes prayer real; you're thinking about the person and you're thinking about the relationship you have with them. And so he says, "Every time I remember you, I thank God for you." So, there's a remembrance; there's a relationship built up. One of the beauties of healthy local church life is to know and be known. You get involved in lives with each other and they know you and you can pray for each other based on remembrance, on actual knowledge that you have. So, Paul has great memories with the Philippians.

And so, we also see his consistency. He is a consistent prayer warrior concerning them. Verse 3-4: "I thank my God *every* time I remember you and *all* my prayers for all of you. I *always* pray with joy." This is consistency language. He didn't just pray once for them and that box was checked. He's just continually praying for them, regularly and consistently praying for them.

We also see his joy in his prayers for them. Paul's prayers for them were characterized by joy. "I always pray with *joy*. You bring me *joy*." He's delighted in the grace of God at work in them, their lives. He loves that relationship. They bring him joy. Philippians is an epistle of joy. You come into joy again and again. "Rejoice in the Lord always" (4:4). The Philippians' conversion, their story and their existence as Christians, brought him joy. And he's looking ahead to the joy they're going to have together in heaven. Because it's "better by far to depart and be with Christ" (1:21). And they're going to experience that too. And so, they've got incredible joy ahead of them, waiting for them. So, there's a joy in his prayer.

And then he gives reasons for his prayer. This characteristic of his prayer life is that he's praying based on certain facts and truths and things that are true about his relationship with the Philippians. So first, their partnership or fellowship in the gospel. Verse 5: "Because of your partnership, your *sharing* in the gospel with me, from the first day until now." And then again in verse 7: "For whether I'm in chains or defending and confirming the gospel, all of you *share* in God's grace with me." So, there's a fellowship in the work of the gospel. No one's on their own in the gospel work around the world. We're part of a grand, glorious body of Christ, the people of God. We're all in this together. There is one work going on around the world, and we share in each other's aspects of it and details. So, they share in Paul's apostolic ministry as a trailblazing, frontier preacher to the Gentiles, planting churches. They share in that through their prayers for him. And so, there's a partnership. But they're also sharing with money. They send money through Epaphroditus. So, they're partnering with him in the gospel, and he gives thanks for them. So, there's that sense of shared experience. And he's also partnering with God and with the Holy Spirit in their ongoing salvation. They're not done being saved. They still have a journey to run. And so, he's sharing in that. There's a sharing and a partnership. And that prayer is characteristic of Paul's prayer, that sense of partnership.

And then secondly, God's absolute sovereignty over their salvation in all respects. Beautifully, in verse 6—very famous verse—absolute confidence in the sovereignty of God in salvation, and also that salvation is a process. It begins with justification (begins with full forgiveness of sins), but then there's a journey to be traveled. They're to work out their salvation with fear and trembling (2:12). They've still got to grow in the grace in the knowledge of Christ, as Peter says (2 Pet 3:18). They've got a journey to travel still. They're not done being saved.

"But," he says in verse 6, "being confident of this, that he who began a good work in you will carry it on to completion until the day of Christ Jesus." There is nothing in the heavenly realms or the earthly that can separate us from the love of God in Christ (Rom 8:38-39). And our salvation is a work of God begun in us by his sovereign grace. And he who began that good work is going to keep working in you until he is finished. And what is finished? It is when you are finally in a glorified, resurrected body surrounded by brothers and sisters from every tribe and language and people and nation, who are also in radiantly glorious, resurrected bodies in a beautiful, resurrected world. That's the finished line. And God's not going to stop working until that's done.

And so, "being *confident* of this..." His prayers for them are based on that confidence. God, you are working in the Philippians, and I know you're going to finish that work. Nothing can stop it.

We also see his affection for them. He dearly loves them. Look at verses 7-8: "It is right for me to feel this way about all of you, since I have you in my heart. For whether I am in chains or defending and confirming the gospel, all of you share in God's grace with me. God can testify how I long for all of you with the affection of Christ Jesus." Paul says, "I don't love you as much as Christ Jesus loves you, but I love you *like* he loves you. And my love for you is actually a subset of his love for you. He's loving you, Philippian Christians, through me right now, through the Spirit. But I love you, and I have that affection for you in Christ Jesus." And so, that motivates his prayer.

So, we see the character of Paul's prayer life. Now, let's look at the content of Paul's prayer life in verses 9-11.

2. The content of Paul's prayer life (1:9-11)

"And this is my prayer: that your love may abound more and more, in knowledge and depth of insight, so that you may be able to discern what is best, and may be pure and blameless until the day of Christ, filled with the fruit of righteousness that comes through Jesus Christ, to the glory and praise of God" (1:9-11). So, here in these verses we can sit at the feet of the great apostle Paul and learn what we should pray for when we pray for each other. I mean, Paul has other prayers, and we should learn from those too. But we can get some truths out of this. "We don't know what we ought to pray for," Romans 8:26 says. The Spirit teaches us. This is him teaching us what to pray for.

You ever have that experience where you want to pray for somebody, but you don't know what to pray? We tend to pray for the tyranny-of-the-urgent type things—the thing that's immediately on their radar screen—like the health issue or some other thing or some financial issue or some final exam that they're getting ready for and all that. And there's nothing wrong with praying for those things, but we've got to pray for these types of themes.

So, he prays that their love may abound more and more. Salvation's all about love. It's all about transforming us so that we will finally and forever fulfill the two great commandments. That God would take out from us our heart of stone and give us a heart of flesh that will finally love like it was meant to love. And what are those two great commandments? You know them well. The first and greatest commandment is this, that you would love the Lord your God with all of your heart, with all of your soul, with all of your mind, and with all of your strength. When you're converted, that love has begun to develop in you, but it's not finished, is it? And then that second command is like it, to love your neighbor as yourself. That you would love God more and more, and that you would love your neighbor more and more, as you already do love yourself.

So, we ask for those things to develop. He's praying, "God, you've begun to work in the Philippian Christians. You've begun to work in their hearts, and they've begun to love you like they should. But that is a long journey yet to go. Would you please, oh Lord, work in them so that they would love you more and more, that their love for you would overflow?" The word is *abound*, that it would be like a fountain overflowing—a passion for Christ, a passion for Christ's Word, a passion for Christ's work in the world, that you would love it more and more, that you'd be on fire for it, that you would not be lukewarm like the Laodiceans that Jesus wants to vomit out of his mouth because they're lukewarm, but rather that they would be passionately loving God and loving others more and more.

And he says, "...in knowledge and depth of insight." Paul wants a perfect unity between head and heart, between doctrine and passion, between light and heat. And it is in that order. Light is truth, and heat is passion about that truth. So, the truth always leads the way. The Word of God always leads the way, as I'm seeking to do now by preaching Philippians 1, that the Word of God would lead the way, the truths would lead and then your passion would come in behind it. And there'd be a combination of truth and heat on fire. So, love without knowledge is emotionalism, sentimentalism, maybe even idolatry. Conversely, knowledge without passion is formalism, and really just a form of hypocrisy. There has to be that beautiful combination of head and heart, of right doctrine and hearts on fire in reference to that doctrine. And that's what he's praying for. And so, he wants that deep knowledge about God in his Word and of God personally.

And then...a sense of discernment. So, he talks about discernment: "that you may be able to discern what is best." Discernment is wisdom. Being able to discern, the author of Hebrews tells us, good from evil. It starts there. You're able to discern good from evil. But then there's other aspects of discernment—that you may be able to approve the things that are excellent (as the American Standard has it in verse 10). Approve those things that are excellent, so that you would be able to see the difference between good, better, and best in the Christian life, and you can see the path that God has specifically for you—what he's calling you to do, and how you're gifted, and what you're called to do to contribute to the kingdom of God. And you can discern that. So yes, definitely discerning good from evil (hating evil), but also discerning good, better, and even best, and approving of those things from your heart. So, Paul wants their love to grow more and more in their knowledge of God and of his Word, with the result that they have a refined ability to discern. They can look over the mass of possibilities and know clearly what God wants them to do. What is the excellent thing God is calling them to do?

And he prays for purity in their lives—holiness, a sense of purity. The outcome of this abounding love and knowledge is a refined discernment to know what is God's best and to delight in it and to live a pure life as a result. Look at verse 10: "so that you may be able to discern what is best, and may be pure and blameless until the day of Christ." The Greek word used here is basically like sun-tested. You can imagine someone making a very expensive vase and holding it up to the light, which is the brightest light they would have had back in Paul's day, to look at. Bright, sunny, noon-day sun. Hold it up and the light comes through it like it's translucent. You can see imperfections. You can see flaws. You can see blemishes. That's the image that he has here. So, he wants them to be pure and blameless until the day of Christ. We are assaulted. Our faith is assaulted. Our souls are assaulted every day by the world, the flesh, and the devil. Every day. We're in a war zone—the lust of the eyes, the lust of the flesh, the pride of life is assaulting us and wants to corrupt us and make us impure. Paul wants the Philippians to stand firm in their pagan culture, and our culture is increasingly pagan. And it's the same temptations that they fought in those days. We have to fight the same—against lust and covetousness and greed and bitterness and anger and unforgiveness, all of these corrupting sins.

He wants them to be pure until the day of Christ Jesus. And he wants them to persevere in that. Think about that. To be pure now and to be pure tomorrow and to be pure a week from now and a year from now and for the rest of your lives—that they would be pure until the day of Christ Jesus. And what is that? What is "the day of Christ Jesus"? It's judgment day. That day is coming for us all. Paul never stopped thinking about it. When he was on trial before Felix, he said, "I strive always to keep my conscience clear before God and man, to not do anything that would violate my conscience" (Acts 24:16). Oh students, I beg you, fight the good fight of faith. Don't violate your conscience. Don't become impure and corrupted and unholy. Someday you're going to have to stand before the judgment seat of Christ, that you may receive from him what is due you for the things you did in the body, whether good or bad (2 Cor 5:10). Paul never forgot about that. "So, I want you, Philippians," he said, "to be pure and blameless until that final day."

Part of my job as a pastor is to remind my people of that coming day. It is coming. And you will have to give an account for everything you've done in the body, whether good or bad. Are you ready? So, Paul wants them to be pure and blameless until that day, persevering in it.

And...fruitful. Look at verse 11: "filled with the fruit of righteousness that comes through Jesus Christ." Fruit of righteousness. So, we need to understand the theology of salvation. We believe in a perfect righteousness required for judgment day, that if you do not have that perfect righteousness, you will not go to heaven but will be condemned to hell. You must be perfect as your heavenly Father is perfect. You must have a perfect righteousness. Paul talks about that perfect righteousness in this very epistle. In Philippians 3:9 he says, "I consider all of my own self-righteousness to be garbage, so that I might be found in Christ, not having a righteousness of my own that comes from the law, but that which is through faith in Christ, the righteousness that comes from God and is by faith." That's the imputed righteousness of justification that happens in an instant the moment you genuinely repent of your sins and believe in Jesus. At that moment, you are seen by God to be as righteous as Jesus Christ himself. Think about that—the imputed righteousness of Christ. On what basis did the thief on the cross go to heaven? His good works? No. But by faith he saw that Jesus was Lord. He said, "Remember me, Lord, when you come into your kingdom." And Jesus said, "Today, you'll be with me in paradise." On what basis? Imputed righteousness, by faith.

But there is a fruit of that righteousness that comes, and that's what he's praying for here. The fruit of righteousness that comes, that's a good life filled with good works—works of holiness, of actually putting lusts to death by the Spirit, works of benevolence, of giving money like they did to Paul's ministry, of being generous with their time and their energy and their money, of leading other people to Christ. He's going to urge them to stand firm in a time of persecution there in Philippi and not to be afraid at all of those who were opposing the gospel but being bold to share the gospel, and shine like lights in a dark age, filled with the fruit of righteousness, the fruit of good works. That's what he wants.

So, we've seen the character of Paul's prayer of life in verses 3-8, and then the content of Paul's prayer of life in verses 9-11. But what is the ultimate goal?

3. The ultimate goal of Paul's prayer life (1:11)

Why do we pray? Well, it's always the same. We don't have to wonder what the goal is or what the ultimate reason is. It's always the same. What is it? The glory of God. Everything we do is for the glory of God. Look at verse 11, at the very end: "to the glory and praise of God." Human salvation is important, very important. It's just not ultimately important. It's not the ultimate reason, right? The ultimate reason for everything is God. It all goes back to how I began this message. It all goes back to God on his throne. God enthroned is everything. And so, our prayers—all of these details and all of these attributes and characteristics—go toward one thing in the end: that God would be glorified and praised because of you and me.

And so, in heaven we're going to celebrate forever the glory of God in the lives of that multitude that was saved from every tribe and language and people and nation, how God saved them, how he began a good work in each of them, what he did to preserve them and protect them and then use them. We're going to spend eternity in heaven learning those things. There's a lot to learn, brothers and sisters. You've got a lot of new friends you're going to meet when you get to heaven. And you're going to find out how God used them. And they're going to find out how God used you and worked in you. And all of it will be for the glory and praise of God.

Didn't Jesus say in Matthew 13:43, "Then the righteous will shine like the sun in the kingdom of their Father"? We're going to shine with radiant glory. But where is that glory coming from? It's not our own glory. We don't originate it. It's all the glory of God in us. As it says again in

Revelation 21, the New Jerusalem shone with the glory of God, and its brilliance was like that of a very precious jewel, like a jasper, clear as crystal. That's where we're heading, and that's where all of our prayers should go. That God would be glorified in that person and that that person would praise God for his glory. That is the purpose.

Conclusion

So, application? Pray like that. Pray like that. Find each other and pray together like this. Say, "I want to pray like Philippians 1:3-11. I want to pray that for you. I want to pray for the glory and praise of God, that God would work in you in this way." Pray like that.

Chapter 2

NO MATTER WHAT

Philippians 1:12-26

Brian Arnold[1]

Introduction

For the last eight years, I had the privilege of teaching church history. In particular, I taught patristics, or the church fathers. What drew me to them was their undaunted zeal for Christ. Most of them in the second century did not have a full Bible, if any of them did. They did not have 2,000 years of Christian witness. Yet they faced unimaginable torture and death for the name of Jesus Christ.

But in teaching history, the lecture that I was always most excited about was the modern missions movement that began at the very end of the eighteenth century and into the nineteenth century, where men and women left everything in this world to go to a foreign mission field— where they served, where they faced deep suffering, and where they died. And the story that has always arrested my attention most is the life and ministry of John Paton.

Paton was a missionary to the New Hebrides, modern day Vanuatu. By the time of his death in 1907, Paton was able to claim that the island was won for Christ. About 3,000 people had turned to Christ in faith, and today about 85% or so of the people there claim Jesus as Lord. But it is the story of how he came to be there in the first place that grips me. John Paton set sail in 1858. Twenty years before he left, two other missionaries had set out to win the New Hebrides for Christ—John Williams and James Harris

---

[1] Brian Arnold is Senior Pastor of First Baptist Church, Paducah, Kentucky.

in 1839. As soon as these two men reached shore, the natives clubbed them to death, roasted their bodies, and ate them.

That should have been it. These people are not open to the gospel. Dust off the sandals and move on. But not Paton. He yearned to go. As he was raising funds to embark on this journey a man named Mr. Dickson exclaimed, "The cannibals! You will be eaten by cannibals!" Paton's response must go down as one of the best in history. Undeterred, and I like to think with a small smirk, he replied:

> Mr. Dickson, you are advanced in years now, and your own prospect is soon to be laid in the grave, there to be eaten by worms; I confess to you, that if I can but live and die serving and honoring the Lord Jesus, it will make no difference to me whether I am eaten by Cannibals or by worms; and in the Great Day my Resurrection body will rise as fair as yours in the likeness of our risen Redeemer.

In between arriving and seeing the island won for Christ, he suffered greatly, perhaps mostly in the death of his wife and newborn son. After burying her, he had to sleep on her grave for fear that the cannibals would dig her up and eat her. Yet he stayed. He soldiered on.

How does a man do that? Paton tells us what got him to go and what kept him there. He said, "Life, any life, would be well spent, under any conceivable conditions in bringing one human soul to know and love and serve God and His Son." That was John Paton's heart. And that was the Apostle Paul's heart. But I am wondering if that heart beats in this room today. Are there people in this room who would say, "My life is well spent, under any conceivable condition, if only I can bring people to Christ." It is what set the world on fire with gospel missions in the nineteenth century. Whether it was William Carey or Adoniram Judson, Amy Carmichael or

Lottie Moon, they had an unquenchable desire to make Christ known no matter what. And I wonder if it will be the same in this generation, or if we will get sidetracked by every little debate and battle that rages. It cost them all dearly, in different ways, but they (like Paul) "did not account their lives of any value nor as precious to themselves, if only they might finish the course and the ministry that they received from the Lord Jesus, to testify to the gospel of the grace of God" (Acts 20:24).

We are in Philippians chapter 1 and Paul is writing from prison. Of all places, Paul should be discouraged. But he isn't. He's right where God wanted him to be, so he has the right disposition of heart that we see in this passage. And his disposition is this, which is my big idea for today—resolve to live a "no-matter-what" life.

That was Paul's resolve. Come what may, no matter what, I will spend my life, I will spend myself, all day, every day for the gospel of Jesus Christ. My concern is that too many Christians live a life more hedged in than that. They want a more comfortable life. Enough to have heaven. Enough to have a nice life. But not a no matter what life.

This resolve of Paul's is evident in all his letters and in the example of his life, but it comes across so poignantly and powerfully in Philippians 1:12–26. Pick up with me in verse 12 under this first main point.

1. Advance the gospel, no matter what (1:12–14)

Let's read Philippians 1:12–14: "I want you to know, brothers, that what has happened to me has really served to advance the gospel, so that it has become known throughout the whole imperial guard and to all the rest that my imprisonment is for Christ. And most of the brothers, having become confident in the Lord by my imprisonment, are much more bold to speak the word without fear."

We aren't for certain about when or where Paul is writing this letter. Most likely he is writing from a prison in Rome in the final years of his life, maybe around AD 62, and history tells us that Paul will be beheaded sometime after the Neronian fires of AD 64. There are guards, the imperial guard which is the prestigious guard of Caesar, and it doesn't take long for them to realize that they are the captives. "What are you in for," checks notes, "Paul?" Paul replies: "For telling people about Jesus. When is your shift over? I've got something to tell you. It'll knock your socks off and change your life!" It's known throughout the whole guard because Paul cannot shut his mouth.

What makes this passage so striking is that Paul completely inverts expectations. Suffering advances the gospel. Imprisonment advances the gospel. The chains that should show the power of Caesar are actually clasped on Paul by Christ so that his glory would be advanced. Because nothing can stop the power of the gospel. And Paul's imprisonment had a twofold opposite reaction: (1) instead of suppressing the gospel, his imprisonment served to expose the praetorian guard to the gospel, and (2) instead of creating fear in other Christians, it emboldened them to share the gospel.

Paul reminds us of this in his valedictory letter, 2 Timothy, that the gospel is never chained (2 Tim 2:9). If Paul learned anything throughout his life of struggle and persecution, it's that God's Word can go forth in any circumstance, *if* we will open our eyes and see these moments as God's given instruments to spread the gospel. His entire argument is that it is the adversity that is advancing the gospel. Had Paul not been put in prison, the gospel would not have gone forth like it did.

Here we see the great irony of persecution—that which is intended to *squelch* the gospel always serves to *spread* the gospel. Paul knew this. He was the persecutor turned persecuted. He had already witnessed how every time you try to extinguish the flame of Christianity, you instead throw gasoline on the fire. Or it's like blowing the dandelion you think is dead—you scatter its seed everywhere. How does someone suffering for the gospel embolden others to share the gospel? We think it would be the opposite. We think that persecution would result in the quieting of the gospel. Courage begets courage; fear begets fear. Does your boldness in the proclamation of the gospel propel others forward in sharing the faith or does your fear deaden other people's proclamation of the gospel?

Just fifty years or so after Paul was martyred, another Christian was headed to Rome to face the same fate—Ignatius of Antioch. Ignatius understood this principle and said, "Christianity is greatest when it is hated by the world" (Ignatius, *Rom* 3.3). In the last century, an enemy of the faith came to realize this as well. Yemelyan Yaroslavsky—a Russian politician, journalist, revolutionary, and militant atheist—was the Chairman of Stalin's "League of the Militant Godless." (If you're looking for a club name, that one's already taken.) He wanted nothing more than to exterminate Christians. And yet he realized this frustrating phenomenon. Persecution makes Christianity grow, not shrink. He once said, "Christianity is like a nail. The harder you strike it the deeper it goes."

When you are hated for your faith, it is the greatest darkness to shine the light. Jesus told Paul how much he would have to suffer. Jesus told his disciples that a servant is not greater than his master—if they persecuted him, they would persecute us. Why would we be surprised when the world, which hates the gospel, responds with vitriol against the saints of God? There is a war going on—and Paul would use anything the enemy threw at him to make much of the gospel. Prison—fine. Suffering—fine. Persecution—fine. You cannot silence this message.

What if it is not persecution? What if, in your case, it is run-of-the-mill suffering? How do you respond in moments of testing? Is it opportunity to share Christ or is it license to get mad at God? The counsel today is to get mad at God—"if this is how God treats his most faithful servants, I'm done." Imagine if Paul had just given into despair. Imagine how that would've spread. Our reaction in times of trial will either inspire our fellow believers to speak boldly about Christ or cause them to shrink back. How is suffering met in your life? Opportunity for God's glory to advance or grumbling and complaining? Lack of faith and dismissal or boldness and confidence? Would you be willing to sign on for these hard life circumstances if you knew it would advance the gospel? When you're 21 and you have cancer—will you use it to advance the gospel and spread boldness? Or will you turn inward with resentment? When you lose your job because you're unwilling to buckle to societal pressure, will you do so rejoicing that Christ might be known through your suffering?

All throughout the New Testament, written on nearly every page, is the realization that God transforms the suffering for his people. We don't glory in the suffering for suffering's sake, we glory in the gospel, and we allow God to use the tool of suffering to draw others in. Nothing speaks louder to this world than a Christian who can glorify God when it hurts. Talk about a magnet for faith!

What is happening to Paul is of secondary importance. Imprisonment doesn't matter. In prison or out of prison, proclaiming Christ is all that counts. And Paul wanted his life to count. He realized that his life only counted in regard to his faithfulness to make much of Christ. Maybe you're the one in your friend group who can get the ball rolling. You will have courage at your job to make Christ known. And your boldness will encourage others to make Christ known. But you have to meet suffering and persecution with a "no matter what" for the gospel heart.

One cost, perhaps a surprising one to Paul, is that he was met with opposition from fellow believers. But his attitude was centered on Christ. Second, we see that we must...

2. Support Christ proclaimed, no matter what (1:15–18)

Philippians 1:15–18: "Some indeed preach Christ from envy and rivalry, but others from good will. The latter do it out of love, knowing that I am put here for the defense of the gospel. The former proclaim Christ out of selfish ambition, not sincerely but thinking to afflict me in my imprisonment. What then? Only that in every way, whether in pretense or in truth, Christ is proclaimed, and in that I rejoice."

Not everyone was in Paul's corner. Some were not inspired by his imprisonment—they used his imprisonment to heap on scorn and shame. Some preach from good will, but others, in every generation, will preach from envy and rivalry. Paul mentions here two hearts from which to share the gospel—sincerity, good will, love; or envy, rivalry, selfish ambition.

Obviously, it is ideal to share Christ from a heart of love. In 2 Corinthians 5 Paul lists numerous motivations for sharing the faith. Timothy Beougher, in fact, identifies ten motivations in his book, *Invitation to Evangelism*. But the greatest of these motivations, in my opinion, is that Christ's love compels us (2 Cor 5:14). It is what Paul prizes here. Some share Christ out of good will—out of love. And that's how we should share the gospel.

Do you have a heart for the lost? Paul can advance the gospel and support Christ proclaimed, no matter what, because he loved Jesus and people. Look, if you don't love people, you can't be effective for Jesus. Jesus is the epitome of love for others. Paul will say in the next chapter that Jesus didn't look to his own interests—he looked to ours, and he became obedient to death, even death on a cross. That's a heart for people. That's love overflowing. But there are others who don't preach from this motivation. Although we don't know precisely whom Paul has in mind here, we do learn something about their character. They are full of envy and rivalry. I love Paul's response. Who cares! Is Christ proclaimed? Is the gospel going forth? Then I support it! Cause them no trouble, don't stand in their way. Only that in *every way* Christ is proclaimed.

"But Paul, they're trying to upstage you?" So what?! It's not about me. It's about Jesus. And if Christ is truly proclaimed, then praise God!

There is a critical distinction we must make here. Paul was fine with their message advancing because they were proclaiming Christ. He had no issue with their message—only their temperament. This is not about heresy. Paul showed us everywhere in his writings that heresy wouldn't be tolerated. This is no tolerance for heresy. Paul had no such tolerance, and neither should we. In Galatians 1 Paul anathematized those who preached a false gospel. Even later in Philippians 3 he warned to watch out for the dogs. These are not the same people. One group is proclaiming Christ but doing so with tainted motives. One is tampering with the gospel. We must not tolerate heresy; but we also must not stand in the way of Christ proclaimed.

There are two points of application we need to see here. First, not everything is heresy. Our problem today is that we've elevated everything to the level of heresy. To disagree on any point of doctrine is to label someone heretical and dismiss them. We have elevated everything to Defcon 1—everything is nuclear preparedness and people are building big ministries as takedown artists. Less time being keyboard warriors tearing down ministries and more being kingdom warriors who share the gospel with the lost! Don't mishear me. I think doctrinal integrity is critical. But I wonder if our barometer for heresy is overly sensitive. I wonder if we spend too much time policing within the ranks and not enough time scattered on mission.

Second, watch out for jealousy. It is easy to be on the side of Paul's oppressor here. There's a lot of jealousy in our midst. Someone who's a little bit smarter and getting more opportunities. Someone who's a better preacher and getting to speak at conferences. Churches that are exploding while yours is plodding. These people were jealous of Paul. In the day of social media and the endless game of comparison, it is so easy to let jealousy and envy take over our hearts even when we most certainly shouldn't—like when it comes to proclaiming the gospel. Let's pray for pure motives. Let's pray for hearts that brim with love. Let's pray for other people's ministry the second that the seed of jealousy begins to take root in our hearts. There is no room for jealousy amongst the servants of the Lord. Only one gets the glory. At the end of it all, let us just be found as faithful servants.

What was the secret to Paul being able to advance the gospel, no matter what, and his ability to support Christ proclaimed, no matter what? It came with his conviction to . . .

3. Live for Christ, no matter what (1:18–26)

Philippians 1:18–26:

> Yes, and I will rejoice, for I know that through your prayers and the help of the Spirit of Jesus Christ this will turn out for my deliverance, as it is my eager expectation and hope that I will not be at all ashamed, but that with full courage now as always Christ will be honored in my body, whether by life or by death. For to me to live is Christ, and to die is gain. If I am to live in the flesh, that means fruitful labor for me. Yet which I shall choose I cannot tell. I am hard pressed between the two. My desire is to depart and be with Christ, for that is far better. But to remain in the flesh is more necessary on your account. Convinced of this, I know that I will remain and continue with you all, for your progress and joy in the faith, so that in me you may have ample cause to glory in Christ Jesus, because of my coming to you again.

This is the culminating point. This is what makes everything he's said so far make sense. And it is in what he says right now, if you get this, and you walk in full agreement with Paul, your life will be radically transformed, and you will be used of Christ to build his kingdom. This is the essence of the Christian life. It is a life that is totally committed to the Lord in life or in death. This is not just for saints like Paul. This is not just for pastors. This is for everyone who calls himself or herself a Christian.

To live is Christ; to die is gain. To live is for fruitful labor. Should I live and should Christ tarry, then everything about my life will be Christ. But should I die, then so be it, I desire that even more because to die in Christ is to see my Savior face to face. And it isn't just a fluke in this letter. It is all over the place in Paul's writings. In Galatians 2:20, Paul wrote, "I have been crucified with Christ. It is no longer I who live, but Christ who lives in me. And the life I now live in the flesh I live by faith in the Son of God, who loved me and gave himself for me." My life is no longer my own. The old me was crucified. The life I now live in the body, I live by faith. Coming to Christ for salvation is a great exchange. His life for mine; my life for his. Or in 2 Corinthians 5:15 where he said, "And he died for all that those who live should no longer live for themselves but for him who for their sake died and was raised."

Paul couldn't be clearer. To be a Christian is to live an exchanged life with the one who exchanged your sins for his righteousness. Now our lives are his. Life? Yes, for his service! Death? Yes, to see him in glory! Part of what Paul is trying to communicate here is that when death is gain, nothing on this earth can stop us or slow us down. The worst they can do is kill us, but death is actually best for us.

> When death is gain . . . we will put other people above our self.
> When death is gain . . . we will consider all things loss for the sake of Christ.
> When death is gain . . . we will live as though our citizenship is in heaven.
> When death is gain . . . we will believe that we can do all things through Christ who gives us strength.

Paul does expect that this imprisonment will not lead to death. He is sure that he will be physically delivered by the prayers of the people and the power of Christ. But I think he also means to convey that he is delivered no matter what, in life or in death. Either way is deliverance; either way is a win.

Is this your heartbeat? I am his. In life, I am his. In death, I am his. In suffering, I am his. Whatever highs or lows, mountain peaks or valleys, I am his—heart, mind, soul, and strength. The obstacle is fear. That is what will keep us from living like this. What are you in fear of? What cripples your heart with anxiety? There is so much freedom in these verses. But, if you're living for this life, then everything that throws you off track, or everything that could throw you off track, will be a source of anxiety and fretting. The reason we so often do not yearn for heaven like Paul is because we've put down too deep of roots here in the present. We need the heart of Charles Spurgeon: "Many there are who carry out this principle in some measure; but who is there that dare say that he hath lived wholly for Christ as the apostle did? Yet, this alone is the true life of a Christian—its source, its sustenance, its fashion, its end, all gathered up in one word—Christ Jesus."

Why is it that we might have a resolve to die for Christ but not live for him? Why does living feel more costly than dying? Dying can be swift. We have heaven to look forward to. But living for Christ requires dying daily. That's why it's harder. It means you're going to have to speak up and speak out for the cause of the kingdom, and that will cost you often. Your reputation will suffer. You may lose a job. You may alienate family. So be it, so long as Christ is magnified! Brothers and sisters, we are called to live by dying daily for Christ.

Conclusion

In 2018, I remember hearing reports of a missionary trying to take the gospel to North Sentinel Island in the Indian Ocean. After a few times of trying to establish contact with the people, he was shot through with a bow and arrow. His name was John Chau. The world heard this news and both jeered at him and derided him as a Christian imperialist who arrogantly tried to tamper with a uncontacted tribe.

My thoughts, like many others, turned to John Paton. Harris and Williams had been killed right away. But Paton didn't care. He said, amazingly, they had baptized the New Hebrides in their blood. Christ was claiming it. And I wondered if there would be someone else who would see North Sentinel Island as baptized in his blood and sense an overwhelming desire to take Christ there. I'll say this—it'll be a person with a "no matter what" faith. A "to live is Christ, to die is gain" attitude.

It may not be that Christ is calling you there. But he is calling you to the places you will work, the places you will live, and the places you will worship. Who will have the "no matter what" life? Who will say that my life counts as nothing if only I might complete the mission that Christ has given to me, the mission of testifying to the gospel of God's grace? Who will pick up the mantle? Who will take the gospel and say, "No matter what?!" I will advance the gospel on the mission field or in the neighborhood or in my profession.

By whatever means, in whatever way, no matter what.

Chapter 3

THE MIND OF CHRIST

Philippians 1:27-2:18

Hershael York[1]

Introduction

The approach that I take to the book of Philippians is what I call a non-linear outline. Throughout Philippians a four-point outline keeps cycling through. Though not always in order, Paul employs four moves throughout the epistle.

First, he talks to the Philippians about *God's purpose* i.e., what God is purposing to do in individuals, in his work, and in history.

Second, Paul emphasizes that *God alone chooses the means to accomplish his purpose*. This is the point at which things get difficult, because sometimes God's means of accomplishing his purpose are inconvenient or painful to us, something we would never choose. For instance, what is God's purpose for Paul? According to 1:12, it is the advance of the gospel. What is the means God chooses to accomplish that purpose in Paul's life? Well, he sticks him in prison. That makes little sense to us. That is not a move any of us would make, nor a church growth step we would likely take. Yet in God's wisdom, he puts his point man in jail.

The third point of this non-linear outline is about our response. *We must respond correctly when God uses any means of his choosing to accomplish his purpose in us*. It is one thing to talk nobly about God's lofty purposes in our lives, but quite another when he is working his purpose in our life

---

[1] Hershael York is Dean of the School of Theology and Victor and Louise Lester Professor of Christian Preaching at The Southern Baptist Theological Seminary in Louisville, Kentucky.

by means we would not choose and do not want. In fact, we often pray for him to remove the very circumstances he has chosen. Yet that is part of his work in our lives. Then the issue becomes, okay, how do I respond to that? Am I responding correctly to the means God has chosen to accomplish his purpose? To look at 1:12 again as an example, Paul says, "I want you to know that the things that have happened to me have happened for the advance of the gospel so that my bonds in Christ are manifest in all the Praetorium and all other places." How is he responding to the fact that he is in jail? There is not one word in the entire book of Philippians by which he calls on the church to contact their senators or to appeal to the emperor to get him out of jail. Instead, he spends his time and ink urging them to respond correctly. God is at work in that means.

Fourth and finally, Paul describes getting the reward, the accomplishment of what God intended all along. *You get the results of your response to God as a means of accomplishing this purpose.* If you do not respond correctly, that purpose gets stunted or short-circuited.

For much of the book of Philippians, Paul highlights *the appropriate response of the believer to the means that God is employing in accomplishing his lofty purposes*. He further mentions the way we reap the results of that response.

Regardless of the place the epistle was penned, Philippians would have been remarkable; however, the verity of it being written by Paul in prison brings an additional significance as Paul is exemplifying the mind of Christ amidst trials and difficult circumstances.

I treasure reading things that men have written under duress. A great example was provided by William Tyndale, the first man to translate the Bible into English. We do not have anything in Tyndale's handwriting except one letter that he wrote from prison. Tyndale was arrested, castigated, reviled, and thrown into a prison for his conviction that ordinary people needed to have the Bible in their own language. Writing from a cold and dingy dungeon that was in a castle in Brussels built in 1374, suffering from the cold, enduring sickness, he wrote to the magistrate:

> I believe, right worshipful, that you are not ignorant of what has been determined concerning me. Therefore, I entreat your Lordship, and that by the Lord Jesus, that if I am to remain here during the winter, you will request the Procurer to be kind enough to send me from my goods, which he has in his possession, a warmer cap, for I suffer extremely from cold in the head, being afflicted with a perpetual catarrh [inflammation in the nose or throat], which is considerably increased in the cell. A warmer coat also, for that which I have is very thin; also a piece of cloth to patch my leggings: my overcoat is worn out; my shirts are also worn out. He has a woolen shirt of mine, if he will be kind enough to send it. I have also, with him, leggings of thicker cloth, for putting on above; he has also warmer caps for wearing at night. I wish also his permission to have a candle in the evening, for it is wearisome to sit alone in the dark.

Note his final request: "But above all, I entreat and beseech your clemency to be urgent with the Procurer that he would kindly permit me to have my Hebrew Bible, Hebrew Grammar, and Hebrew Dictionary, that I may spend my time with that study. And in return, may you obtain your dearest wish, provided it is always consistent with the salvation of your soul."

Isn't that remarkable? Although he is in the prison for translating the Bible and suffering greatly, he says above all, if you'd be so kind to send me a Hebrew Bible and dictionary, a pen and some paper so that I can keep doing the very thing I got arrested for, so that people can have the word of God! It reveals the heart of a man that genuinely puts the will of God first.

Paul is teaching us to do precisely this. He says, "Beloved! I want you to have a life worthy of the gospel."

Having talked about his own imprisonment, Paul very quickly pivots to their situation in 1:27 by urging them to live a life worthy of the gospel. He is not saying that living the right life makes you worthy of God's salvation—you could never be worthy of what Jesus Christ has done for you! That is why it is of grace. However, upon redemption, one ought to walk and live in a manner that is worthy of the calling and be worthy of the name Christian. If you claim to be a follower of Jesus, you need to live like it.

What does living as a follower of Jesus look like?

First of all, it is about *consistency*; Paul told the Philippians that they need to live this way "whether I'm with you or absent" (1:27).

Secondly, it is about *contending*. The Christian life is a life of constant battle wherein we wage a war against the unholy trinity consisting of the flesh, the world, and the devil. Paul further says that he wants the Philippian church to be contending always for that faith, having courage in the work of God. He exhorts them not to be frightened of anything by their opponents. He further reminds them that this courage will have an effect on those around them. To those who are unbelievers, the godly life lived by believers is a sign of their own condemnation. When we do not fear the world or whatever the world calls us or throws at us, but instead have a confident trust in the God who puts us in that circumstance, it is a testimony to others. Your courage will encourage other believers and condemn unbelievers. It is needed because "it has been granted to you that for the sake of Christ you should not only believe in him but also suffer for his sake" (1:29).

Frankly, we do not like that word. Our hearts thrill to the part about believing. It has been given to me to *believe*. Yes, faith is a gift, to be sure.

But my circumstances are every bit as much a gift of God as my faith!

Paul wrote this epistle from a prison cell; I am sure you have some circumstances that have imprisoned you. There is something in your life that you did not ask for. It is not a result of your sin or bad decisions; it is just circumstances you are stuck with. It might be some physical issue, it might be your background, it might be the circumstances of your birth, your life, something you struggle with. You would give anything for God just to take that away. If he could just one day do a miracle and take away those circumstances, you would think you could serve him better.

But what Paul is reminding us of is that suffering in your life is as much a gift as the very faith that God has used to save you. It is granted to you on behalf of Christ, not only to believe, but also to suffer. This is what living a life worthy of the gospel looks like. We should not be angry with God or resentful because he does not make our lives easier. This is where Paul transitions in chapter 2, indicating that, following a crucified Savior, not only should we live a life worthy of the gospel, but we should also cultivate a mind humbled by Christ Jesus.

In chapter 2, with incredible pastoral skill, he says there is something you can do for me: "So if there is any encouragement in Christ, any comfort from love, any participation in the Spirit, any affection and sympathy, complete my joy by being of the same mind, having the same love, being in full accord and of one mind" (2:1-2).

The first sentence in this chapter is conditional and somewhat unusual. It has four protases (conditional clauses) and one apodosis (the main clause). He uses four "ifs" to introduce his request. How can we do that, Paul? By being of the same mind, having the same love, being in full accord, and in one mind. This is what a good pastor does. Dr. Van Neste mentioned that I completed twenty years at Buck Run Baptist Church and stepped down as senior pastor last Sunday. About two years ago, we decided that by January 24, I would step down, and my associate pastor of nine years would succeed me as senior pastor. We termed it a "no drama, no trauma" transition. Many churches do not experience such smooth transitions; they encounter drama and trauma. We aimed to avoid that. When asked, "Dr. York, is there anything you wish to say to us in your final message?" I replied, "There is something you can do for me. Follow Chris Parrish as your senior pastor, who will continue to preach the gospel." I stated that if the name Hershael York were never mentioned again at Buck Run Baptist Church, but the name of Jesus Christ was exalted until his return, I would be content.

This is what Paul is saying: "There is something you can do for me." What is it, Paul? "Get your act together. Pursue unity and stop being divided." A mind humbled by Christ Jesus is marked by unity and humility.

Paul instructs them to prioritize others over themselves. Imagine if Christians genuinely lived this way. It would be countercultural. Yet, I fear we have become a group of selfish, angry people whom the world might view with disdain. This is contrary to Paul's teaching. Do not seek only your own interests but the interests of others. Place others before yourself and advance others before advancing yourself.

We might respond, "Paul, that is so difficult to do. How can I achieve this?" He answers, "Let this mind be in you, which is yours in Christ Jesus" (2:5). Some translations say, "which was also in Christ Jesus" or "in Jesus." Regardless, the point remains the same: you need the mind of Christ. It is available to you. Peter says, "His divine power has granted to us all things that pertain to life and godliness, through the knowledge of him who called us to his own glory and excellence" (2 Peter 1:3). Thus, since you have access to the mind of Christ, you must think like Christ.

What did Christ do? "Though he was in the form of God, he did not regard equality with God as something to be grasped" (2:6). This does not infer that he gave up his attributes or the essence of being God. He was always fully God, even as a baby in a manger. But, he gave up the rights and prerogatives of divinity. He did not cling to his divine status. He left his Father's throne where angels worshiped him continually, singing, "Holy, Holy, Holy!" to be constrained in a human body inhabiting a dirty world. He humbled himself, taking on the form of a servant, but not merely any servant. Angels are servants, but he became lower than the angels. He assumed the form of a man and was born in the likeness of men. He was not merely a great man; he was an obedient man, obedient even to the point of death, not to an ordinary death but to a cruel execution of crucifixion.

Do you see the downward steps our Savior took? Paul is saying, "Let that mind be in you." Embrace humility and intentionality. This is not achieved by accident and is not natural. It requires daily appropriation of the mind of Christ. We respond with the mind of Christ, remembering that Jesus emptied himself. When we feel that little rise of irritation, aggravation, even anger, because someone has mistreated us, we remind ourselves the way our Savior lived and the way he is calling us to live. We often speak of being servants until we are treated as one, at which point we resist. We stand up for our rights, responding that they cannot treat us in a certain way. But Jesus remained obedient, even to the death of the cross. Because of this, God highly exalted him (2:9). Notice that Jesus endured the cross before receiving the crown. He was crucified before being coronated. We often wish to skip the cross and go straight to the crown. We desire to sit at the right hand of the Father but shy away from rejection by men. However, God exalted Jesus because of his obedient life.

Now, building on that, Paul says in the third section that you have to have a salvation that is worked out in obedience. "Therefore, my beloved, as you have always obeyed, so now, not only as in my presence but much more in my absence" (2:12). He is pointing back to what he said in 1:27 where he reminded them to have consistency; it is not about when one of your professors or pastors or another Christian is watching you. Because what you are in secret is what you are. You need to be holy in secret. You need to be fully committed to the Lord alone or around people. It just should not matter. Your character should be rooted in Christ, not who is watching. So, Paul says, work out your own salvation with fear and trembling, work out your own salvation with fear and trembling, for it is God who works in you, both to will and to work for his good pleasure (2:12-13).

Paul exhorted us to be courageous. He further reminds us that working *out* the salvation that God has worked *in*, is serious business. He does not mean that we go through life fearful, quaking that God is going to throw a lightning bolt at us because we messed up. But he is saying that this is serious. Just as we expect serious commitment from professionals like airplane mechanics or brain surgeons, God expects us to take our salvation seriously. It is not a part of who you are; it consumes you; it is who you are. How do you show that? Look at verse 14. "Do all things without grumbling or disputing." Wow! That is hard. I'm a grumbler by nature. I tell my wife Tanya, "I'm a lovable curmudgeon." And she responds, "No! You do not get to do that. You certainly do not get to call yourself that."

Paul says, "Do all things without grumbling or disputing." This can be challenging. When faced with circumstances like dealing with poor customer service, do you remain kind or do you become irritated? Paul instructs us to avoid grumbling and disputing. This behavior marks us to be blameless and innocent, as children of God without blemish, in the midst of a crooked and twisted generation. It is this behavior that makes us shine as lights in the world (2:15).

Paul says, "I'm ready to die. I might be poured out like a drink offering" (2:17). Well, the Greeks would pour out part of their drink before taking a drink of something. It was called libation, and they would say it was to the gods. Paul says, "My very life is about to be poured out like a drink offering, and my hope is that I've not been sacrificed in vain because you are not living out the salvation that God has worked in you."

We all fantasize about the outworking of our faith, thinking about scenarios wherein a band of men attack us with guns, demanding us to recant our faith in Christ or face martyrdom. We dream that we would never turn our backs on Jesus, fantasizing that we will boldly make a confession of faith in Christ and not deny him before men, thus being prepared to face consequences for faith in Christ, and one day a plaque would be put up saying that Hershael York was here, who was martyred for faith. Well, we suppose that we can handle the pressure. Can you handle not being a grump? Can you do that for Jesus?

We are probably not going to be martyred for our faith in the way I described it, but every day of our life we are called not to grumble and dispute and show ourselves to be completely different like the Savior who was obedient even to the death of the cross. Do not let the irritations, the aggravations, the circumstances of life rob you of your Christ-likeness.

This mind of Christ, it is yours. Have that mind. Shine as lights in the world. Be different because you do not grow old. You do not grow old. You are so possessed of the humility of Jesus and so different from the world around you that you shine as a light to the glory of God.

Chapter 4

UNUSUALLY USEFUL
FOR CHRIST

Philippians 2:19-30

Ken Lewis[1]

Introduction

Thank you. Thanks be to God our Father, to Christ our Savior, to the Holy Spirit who is our Comforter.

It is good to be here with you on this morning. I want to thank and give honor to the leadership here at Union University: to Dr. Oliver, to his cabinet, the leadership; and to Dr. Van Neste for the invitation given to me to stand and to bring God's Word today to you in chapel.

I tell you what, I am really excited to be here for the first time to preach. The last time I preached in a chapel service, I had to look at least four or five rows back to see a face. And you all are in here on the front rows and filling in throughout the room.

So, I'm grateful that you're here and ready to hear God's Word; or at least you're ready to get chapel done and move on. But you are here, and we're grateful that you are here, and we are certainly joyful to be in this place today. I bring you greetings from the Memphis College of Urban and Theological Studies, your colleagues in Midtown Memphis. And we are excited just to be a part of the Union family. Union is well represented in Memphis and carrying on the business of Christ-centered education in that city. So, we certainly are grateful to connect with the main campus

---

[1] Ken Lewis is Dean of the Memphis College of Urban and Theological Studies (MCUTS) at Union University and Senior Pastor of Briarwood Church, Memphis, Tennessee.

whenever we can, but this is a wonderful day to do that as we worship our Lord together.

Well, my business here is to preach God's Word. I'm going to ask that you turn with me to the book of Philippians. I am the next messenger in this series of messages through this wonderful letter, as you have been hearing other messages up to this point in a consecutive expository treatment of this letter that Paul wrote to the church in Philippi.

The text for this morning will be from Philippians 2:19–30 (NKJV). The Word of God reads as follows:

> But I trust in the Lord Jesus to send Timothy to you shortly, that I also may be encouraged when I know your state. For I have no one like-minded, who will sincerely care for your state. For all seek their own, not the things which are of Christ Jesus. But you know his proven character, that as a son with his father he served with me in the gospel. Therefore I hope to send him at once, as soon as I see how it goes with me. But I trust in the Lord that I myself shall also come shortly.
>
> Yet I considered it necessary to send to you Epaphroditus, my brother, fellow worker, and fellow soldier, but your messenger and the one who ministered to my need; since he was longing for you all, and was distressed because you had heard that he was sick. For indeed he was sick almost unto death; but God had mercy on him, and not only on him but on me also, lest I should have sorrow upon sorrow. Therefore I sent him the more eagerly, that when you see him again you may rejoice, and I may be less sorrowful. Receive him therefore in the Lord with all gladness, and hold such men in esteem; because for the work of Christ he came close to death, not regarding his life, to supply what was lacking in your service toward me.

In his bestselling book entitled *Outliers*, Malcolm Gladwell looked at those who were considered the best and the brightest in their respective crafts. He focused on those that were called overachievers. He wanted to see how they were different from others. In other words, why were they outliers? He did not just look at the end result of their success as we would so often observe. We would become fixated on the end game so to speak.

But Gladwell wanted to see what brought them here, what were the character traits, what were the habits, what was their journey to get to the place of success. In other words, he did not just show their glory, he told their story. What he proved here is that success was often attributed to doing these unusual things, these even undesirable things, in a consistent and repeated basis over time that eventually rolled up into a moment of success, a moment of expertise, a moment of accomplishment. In other words, a person becomes an outlier by being consistently better and growing in whatever they do.

Well, Paul here spoke well of two Christian outliers, Timothy and Epaphroditus. These were two humble servants who were unusually useful. That's how I've labeled them. They were unusually useful for Christ and his church. They stood out, not because they were supremely talented or they were highly accomplished. But they stood out because they did what many considered "little things" very well and consistently. They were humble in their service to Christ.

As you have been hearing messages through the book of Philippians, you have learned that in Philippians 2, Paul here is presenting a picture of unity for the church. And he shows that if there's going to be spiritual unity, there has to be selfless humility. He presents Jesus as the ultimate example of one who considered others' needs of more importance than his own. In that gospel story, in that message we see in Philippians 2:5–11, he presents Christ as the one who divested himself of heavenly glory to come to earth so that that we may reap the benefits of his sacrificial service for us.

Well, Jesus is God and completely perfect. We can agree to that. And you may say, "Well, Jesus can do that, but I'm not Jesus. I can't have that kind of mind, or that's too high of a goal from me."

But what Paul does here is he puts two regular, run-of-the-mill guys before us and presents them as heroes of the faith because they would be humble servants to the Lord Jesus Christ. And I believe what Paul shows us here in these two men is that if Timothy and Epaphroditus can be outliers in the Christian faith, that gives hope for all of us. Even if we don't have a large platform, even if we don't write 70 books that are *New York Times* bestsellers, even if we don't speak in all of the continents around the world, we can still stand out and be outliers for the Lord Jesus Christ by being humble servants for him.

We can relate to these men. They had everyday responsibilities. They had challenges. They had adversity—things that all of us experience, but they still were highlighted here.

I can imagine that these two men had no idea that part of their lives and work would be in-Scripturated for us to see some 2,000 years later as they were just going about their business of serving Christ. But let me tell you something. The Lord does not lose anything that is done to glorify his name. He keeps track. He keeps record of what we do for him. You may think, "Well, I'm just showing up here and I'm trying to do my best to survive and it's hard and there are late nights and there are struggles." But there's hope in doing even what are considered "the little things" and trusting in a big God.

A surface reading of this text would make it seem like Paul is just making travel arrangements. He is being something of a travel agent to Timothy and Epaphroditus on their way. But instead, he informs the church (and us) how these two men were unusually useful for Jesus Christ. And a takeaway for us is that we can be unusually useful for Christ when Christ is preeminent in our lives and his purposes are our priorities.

So, what do we learn from these brothers' humble service to Christ and his church as we seek to be unusually useful as they were? Well, we can see that they were, and we should be, genuinely concerned for the church of Christ.

1. Be genuinely concerned for the church of Christ (2:19–24)

We should be genuinely concerned for the church of Jesus Christ. How would they show this genuine concern? They would show it through their sincerity. Paul was sincerely concerned about the church in Philippi. Timothy shared Paul's heart in having such a concern.

Paul, who I call that "gospel globetrotter," made his way to Philippi on his second missionary journey. And while there, God did a great work, raised up a strong church. It wasn't a large church to be very specific, but it was a faithful church. It was a spiritual church. It was a powerful church. And Paul, having moved on, and now on lockdown in Roman detention, is still concerned about the well-being of this church. Timothy, there with Paul, is also concerned that this church would be doing well.

And of course, the church in Philippi was not unique in that way. Paul was concerned about all the churches, but he was concerned about this church in particular. And so, he stated that he intends at some point to visit with them. Think about how encouraging this would be. The apostle Paul, with all that he has facing him—he has a trial before the Caesar, who at that time was Nero. It could turn out to his death, to his execution, or he could be released, which I believe he was. "Paul, you should have enough to be concerned about where you are. You should be praying hard to be released or for Nero to have a change of heart and to be kind and favorable toward you. Paul, you should be trying to just get to the next day, find a way to make meaning of life being confined into a Roman guard day in and day out." But Paul is concerned for the church. So, the church, having received a message that Paul is concerned for them, would be encouraged to know even with all he's going through that Paul is still concerned about them.

But Paul would also be encouraged because as he hears about them still being faithful to Jesus Christ, he would realize that he doesn't have to be there to hold their hands for them to live as mature Christians. Those of us as parents, we know that very well. We thank God for the time that our children can "adult it," right? They can be mature and make a decision without us having to be there to hold their hands. The church wants to be encouraging to the apostle Paul.

Oh, that we would catch just a portion of this passion that Paul has for the church of Jesus Christ. Well, Timothy—how is it that Timothy could have such a heart as Paul would have? The Scripture tells us here that Timothy was like-minded—similar mind as Paul concerning the church.

That word "like-minded" is a strong word there. The word picture is of someone who has equal soul. They are of the same soul concerning this matter. I find this interesting that here we have the apostle Paul, an older Hellenistic Jew being like-minded with a younger, bi-racial, Jew- Gentile. How can that be? Well, it is the unifying power of the gospel and concern for the Lord Jesus Christ and his glory. We can be different in so many superficial ways, but there's something of which we can all be like minded, and that is the gospel of Jesus Christ and the flourishing and the mission of the church that we have been given. Timothy, like Paul, was genuinely concerned for the church of Jesus Christ.

The question for you this morning, the question for all of us is, "What is your level of concern for the church of Christ?" Just to remind you, you do know that church didn't just sort of emerge from some idea to have a non-profit organization to do good in society? The church was on the heart of Jesus Christ. It was his vision that he provided, that he gave on the rock of the confession that Peter gave. Christ would build the church. He would build his church. Christ is with his church, and Christ is for his church. And if we are for Christ, then we should be for his church.

Perhaps being at a Christian school and having to attend chapel twice a week, you may reason, "That's close enough to church for me." You may reason, "I'll just take my Sundays and sleep in." But I want to encourage you that while this is a great place to be (you really are blessed to be at a school where you can take time out of your day to come and worship and sing and to hear God's Word. I wish I would have been wise enough to make that decision when I was your age, when I went to university. But even though that is good, and it is great for you to have that privilege), this is not the church. This is not the assembly of God's people whose purpose is to come together for worship and to glorify Christ, to make disciples, to be on mission for Jesus. Every one of you needs the local church.

But also, if you are a believer in Jesus Christ, the local church needs you. As a pastor, I know, of course, you know what the trends are in many of our churches. It's just a much better gathering of the people of God when everybody there is not my age and older. Not that I'm all that old. But anyway, young and old, right? There's something beautiful about not just that ethnic mosaic, but that generational mosaic in the body of Christ. You add great value to the church where you are, where you are in this stage and age of life. So, I would encourage you to find a Christ-exalting, gospel-proclaiming, disciple-making, mission-sending church and plant yourself there until God moves you.

Great things will happen. Caring for what matters to Christ is to care about the church, to care about Christians. We serve God, and when we serve God, we serve others.

What made these men unusually useful was not all about their ability but watch this—their availability. The other way in which they show genuine concern for the Church of Christ is through their availability.

Timothy and Epaphroditus, both of them, were ready to make an 800-mile journey from Rome to Philippi. This would be a long and treacherous trip. It would take about six weeks, that is, if everything went well. It would be fraught with danger. They were willing and they were available to do this. If they were seeking their own interests, they would say, "Well, I'm good."

I believe this is why Paul said there was no one else like-minded. Because although there were good Christians in Rome, and he mentions many of them when you read the end of the book of Romans, there were still too many of them that effectively said, "Paul, I'm for the gospel, I'm for the mission and everything, but just give me something else to do besides travel to Philippi." There were not many takers for this mission, but these two were available to the Lord Jesus Christ.

Will you be available? Being used by the Lord is not all about ability. It's really more about your availability. Will you make time? Will you make Christ a priority in your life? You are getting a great education here—world class, top notch—but don't set Christ aside. Let Christ be centric even in what you are doing here.

Even as you are preparing for your vocations, you want to serve God in those respective spaces because God is Lord of all. He wants to use you in whatever occasion he calls you into. Be available to be used by God. I need to hurry on here, as I don't have my normal slate of time on Sunday mornings at Briarwood Church.

But we need to be genuinely concerned for the Church of Christ through sincerity and availability.

But also, what Epaphroditus and Timothy show us here is that we should be steadfastly committed to the cause of Christ.

2. Be steadfastly committed to the cause of Christ (2:25–30)

Be committed, first of all, by dependability. Paul thought to send Timothy, but he would need to hold on to Timothy for just a little while longer. But he's instead going to send Epaphroditus. Who is Epaphroditus? Well, it is believed that Epaphroditus was from Philippi. He was one of their own. He had been sent from Philippi, made the long journey to Rome, to take some needful provisions to the apostle Paul. And Paul considered him as his brother, fellow worker, fellow soldier, your messenger, the one who ministered to my need.

This was a picture of dependability. He could be trusted. Epaphroditus was going to fulfill the mission. He was not going to stop short of doing that which he was given to do.

Oftentimes we can have intentions to start out and to fulfill a goal. And then we find out that it is harder than we thought. You know, like one of those projects you watch on YouTube. When they do it, they make it look so easy. I'm like, "I can do that. Look how easy it was for him." Then you tackle that project. Maybe it's a construction project at home or maybe working on the vehicle or whatever, and you get into it and you've got all these pieces and parts everywhere, then you realize you're lost. You conclude, "I don't know what I'm doing. This is not as easy as I thought it was." And maybe you bail out. Then you call somebody who can help you. You call a carpenter, or you call a mechanic.

But what Epaphroditus proved here is that he would follow through. He would keep on until the end. He was dependable. He was faithful and committed to the cause of Christ in his dependability.

While Epaphroditus was imminently useful to Paul, we also know that he was committed to the community, to the faith community, to the church community. He prioritized his relationships because he wanted to, he needed to, go home. Although he wanted to be with Paul, he understood the need to go home and to take care of things there.

This is living out the gospel. He's embodying what Paul said in Philippians 2:4, to "let each of you look out not only for his own interests, but also for the interests of others." This is the mind of Christ, and it should be the mind of Christians. Epaphroditus was firmly committed to the cause of Christ through dependability, but he was also committed through adversity.

This is important. Epaphroditus evidently took sick while on his mission. He was sick almost to death. Here was one of God's choice servants suffering from sickness. We don't know what the sickness was, but it brought him to the brink of death to the point where Paul mentioned it twice in this text. And this is something that we need to face—the reality of serving is that there is no guarantee that when you serve Christ, that all your circumstances will be exactly as you desire them to be. There's no guarantee you won't get sick. There's no guarantee you won't fail a test. There's no guarantee you won't have setbacks. There's no guarantee you won't be betrayed. There's no guarantee that you won't have to wonder if you're in the right place doing the right thing at the right time. There's no guarantee. The call to Christian service is no guarantee to be trouble free.

The second note about suffering in serving God is that the outcomes are all in God's hands. Paul said that God had mercy on him in healing Epaphroditus. With even having God's mercy on himself, Paul realized that God had shown mercy to Epaphroditus, because Paul, with enough sorrow and troubles, didn't want to have to suffer the grief of losing a beloved brother and friend.

So, while he wasn't instantaneously healed, he was sustained by God and eventually restored by him.

Listen, listen, there was nothing deficient in Epaphroditus' faith because he was sick. There was nothing deficient in Paul's faith because his friend was sick. Listen, there's nothing deficient in our faith when we are dependent upon the Lord. Nothing deficient here. These are faithful servants who sought the Lord Jesus Christ.

"He came close to death, not regarding his life to supply what was lacking in your service toward me," Paul says. This term that's translated "not regarding" is a fascinating term because in the Greek text it is a gambling term. So, if you would ask the question, "Is gambling in the Bible?", here we go. We got gambling in the Bible. Now it doesn't mean you go and install your gambling app and go forward, right? It's not that. That's not the application here. We got a higher application, alright? This word here, it has the idea to throw down a stake to venture.

It carries the idea of being rash or reckless. Epaphroditus seemingly exposed his life in a reckless way. He is what I call a "gospel gambler." He took a risk for Christ. Epaphroditus was thinking about the needs of others, serving to the point where it almost cost him his life.

Will you take a risk for Christ? Will you take a risk to be a part of this church where relationships are not always amenable? Sometimes, you have to deal with conflict. Will you take a risk of doing something where you may not be appreciated? Will you take a risk to do something that maybe won't turn out the way that you expect? But when you take a risk to serve Christ, what kind of risk will you take to serve him and his people? Will you risk pursuing anything that has relational and vocational challenges?

But knowing this, that if you serve Christ, you will serve well. And to serve Christ well, it will serve you well. We serve Christ well when we serve each other in Christ.

Conclusion

So, my friends, to be unusually useful for Christ is to make him preeminent and to make his purposes your priority in life.

Be genuinely concerned for the Church of Christ through sincerity and with availability.

Be steadfastly committed to the cause of Christ with dependability and through adversity.

The gospel—it is worth the gamble. Epaphroditus, he traveled from Philippi to Rome to serve Paul; he would also travel from Rome to Philippi to serve his people. But Christ traveled from heaven to earth to save us. Epaphroditus almost died then, but Jesus did die when he came. While the Lord spared Epaphroditus from his sickness and serving, the Lord did not spare his Son but gave him up for us all. Epaphroditus risked his life for others, but Jesus Christ gave his life for us.

And here is the takeaway as I close. It is this—it's to be all-in for Jesus and go all-out for Jesus. Be all-in for Jesus and go all-out for Jesus. When you do that, you will grow to be the disciple who will be unusually useful for Christ and his cause.

Chapter 5

THE FOUNT OF UNRIVALED JOY

Philippians 3:1-21

Justin Perry[1]

Introduction

Good morning. It is a joy and a privilege to be back on this campus. Many people and many moments on this campus have shaped me into who I am today. In fact, I loved this place so much that I completed my four-year degree in four and a half years.

It's also a joy to see several of you who have been to Tampa over the years participating in our partnership with Union through Go Trips. The influence this school has had on my life did not end when I graduated but has continued through sending you, the students of Union, to Tampa to invest in my family, our church family, and the city that I love. I thank God for the partnership we have in this gospel work. I'm praying that the gospel seeds we sow together, in our weakness, across Tampa Bay would be raised up powerfully into a harvest of spiritual fruit.

I thank God for Union University. I thank God for the commitment Union has to see God's Word rightly taught, understood, esteemed, and proclaimed. Dr. Van Neste, Dr. Wainscott, and Julie [Bradfield], I'm very thankful for the opportunity to be here.

I invite you to open your Bibles to Philippians chapter 3. I'm going to read our passage and then pause to ask God to bless the preaching of his Word.

---

[1] Justin Perry is Lead Pastor of Covenant Life Church, Tampa, Florida.

Finally, my brothers, rejoice in the Lord. To write the same things to you is no trouble to me and is safe for you.

Look out for the dogs, look out for the evil doers, look out for those who mutilate the flesh. For we are the circumcision, who worship by the Spirit of God and glory in Christ Jesus and put no confidence in the flesh. Though I myself have reason for confidence in the flesh also. If anyone thinks he has reason for confidence in the flesh, I have more. Circumcised on the eighth day of the people of Israel, of the tribe of Benjamin, the Hebrew of Hebrews, as to the law of Pharisee, as to zeal, a persecutor of the church, as to righteousness under the law, blameless. But whatever gain I had, I counted as loss for the sake of Christ. Indeed, I count everything as lost because of the surpassing worth of knowing Christ Jesus my Lord. For his sake I have suffered the loss of all things and count them as rubbish in order that I may gain Christ and be found in him, not having a righteousness of my own that comes from the law, but that which comes through faith in Christ, the righteousness from God that depends on faith, that I may know him in the power of his resurrection, and may share his sufferings, becoming like him in his death, that by any means possible, I may attain the resurrection from the dead.

Not that I have already obtained this, or am already perfect, but I press on to make it my own because Christ Jesus has made me his own. Brothers, I do not consider that I have made it my own. But one thing I do: forgetting what lies behind and straining forward to what lies ahead, I press on toward the goal for the prize of the upward call of God in Christ Jesus. Let those of us who are mature think this way, and if in anything you think otherwise, God will reveal that also to you. Only let us hold true to what we have attained.

Brothers, join in imitating me. And keep your eyes on those who walk according to the example you have in us. For many, of whom I have often told you and now tell you even with tears, walk as enemies of the cross of Christ. Their end is destruction, their God is their belly, and they glory in their shame, with minds set on earthly things. But our citizenship is in heaven and from it we await a Savior, the Lord Jesus Christ, who will transform our lowly body to be like his glorious body, by the power that enables him even to subject all things to himself.

I believe that God desires his people to be genuinely happy. Not necessarily happy in the ways that we may want to define happiness, but for us to have a joy that is beyond this world and is able to endure the broken circumstances of this world. I also believe that God purposes to raise up men and women in his church whose lives would count for his glory on the landscape of human history. I believe he desires these things for us this morning. I trust that we too desire these things at a foundational level. I trust that we desire to know and experience happiness that is able to withstand the brokenness in this world and that transcends the circumstances of life. I also trust that it is our ambition to have our lives count for God's glory. Who among us wakens in the morning merely to say, "Lord, help me be mediocre. I just hope to barely exist today. I want to live in such a way as to where no one ever remembers who I am and no one ever cares about what I've done."?

I trust you don't desire that kind of existence. If that is your desire, I would encourage you to talk to someone about the joy that can be found in living fully awakened to God's good design and purposes.

The question before us is this: if God wants unwavering joy for us and he desires that our lives would count for his glory throughout human history—and if that is what we fundamentally desire as well—how do we lay hold of that? Before answering this question, let's evaluate our lives. A few extenuating circumstances or seasons aside, we live our lives from a basic posture that pursues happiness and meaningfulness. The rhythms of your day and patterns of your life are as such because you believe that they are ways of laying hold of joy and purpose.

I believe it is helpful for us to evaluate both our belief and practice as it pertains to finding joy and purpose in life. As one of my seminary professors, Mark Liederbach, used to say, and I trust this is a helpful diagnostic, "Your stated belief plus your actual practice equals your actual belief."

Paul wrote to the Philippians to help them lay hold of God's design for life in Christ. His words in Philippians 3 will likewise help us lay hold of his desire for us to know happiness and for us to live in such a way that our lives would count for his glory. To help us see this, we will consider five encouragements from Philippians 3.

1. Rejoice in the Lord (3:1)

Paul begins this chapter with the word *Finally*, but don't be fooled because he still has much to say. Paul is clear about the basis for their rejoicing. The Philippians were not to rejoice in who they were or what they could do. They are called to rejoice in the Lord. The source of their rejoicing and the impetus for their joy was to be fully in the Lord. This call to rejoice in the Lord is a major thread that runs throughout this small letter. It is an ambition that Paul has for all the churches he ministers to, and it informs how Paul views his ministry to these churches. He was a worker for their joy: "Not that we lord it over your faith, but are workers with you for your joy; for in your faith you are standing firm" (2 Cor 1:24). This wasn't just a truth that Paul wanted other Christians to believe and experience, but he himself modeled this kind of joy in the Lord. Philippians 1:4, 18, and 2:17-18 reveal that though he suffered more than anyone else in this letter, Paul also rejoiced more than anyone else in this letter. He has a joy that is beyond this world and that is not constrained by the circumstances of his life.

In the next chapter, he will say, "Rejoice in the Lord always, again will say rejoice" (Phil 4:4). There are no vacations from joy. No timeouts from rejoicing. Even as he sits in a prison cell unsure of when he will take his last breath, Paul knows unwavering joy. If you are a follower of Jesus, this is what your union with Christ has secured for you—the ability to experience fullness of joy regardless of your circumstances. To be clear, there are very real reasons to feel and experience pain, to have unbelievable heartache, to be acquainted with grief, and to know what it's like to cry yourself to sleep at night. There are real reasons to lament suffering, pain, brokenness, and trial, but in Christ hardships do not keep us from joy. If they did, then Philippians 4:4 would be a cruel command that we would be unable to obey.

If you are not a follower of Jesus, this is perhaps why finding lasting joy has been so elusive to you, because you're looking for it in places that can't deliver what it's promising. Only Christ can provide a joy that exceeds and surpasses the difficulties and the circumstances of this life. Oh, that you would see and believe that what God has designed and what you long for cannot be attained apart from him. We are in great need of Christ.

Philippians 3:1 also announces to us that there is more joy to be had in the Lord than we are currently experiencing. Jesus is truly an inexhaustible fountain of the joy! While these believers know this to be true, Paul gladly takes the opportunity to remind them of this truth. How precious and needed is the ministry of reminders. There is a great temptation to think that "new" is superior to "old," or that unoriginality equals irrelevant. Friends, I gladly remind you that your joy and a life well spent for the glory of God will only happen through countless reminders of the things you already know. The Psalms are filled with such reminders. For example, in

Psalm 77, the turn from despair to hope happens when the psalmist writes, "I will remember the deeds of the Lord; I will remember your wonders of old" (Psalm 77:11). One of the great enemies of your experience of joy is forgetting God and his promises. Friends, immerse yourself in reminders. Encourage your friends to remind you of truths about God that you already know. Prioritize a church that will commit to faithfulness to the old, old story of who Jesus is and what he has done.

Friends, rejoice in the Lord. You say, "Okay, pastor, that sounds good, but that seems far removed from where I find myself today. How do I get there?" I'm glad you asked. Let's consider the second encouragement.

2. Put no confidence in the flesh (3:2-7)

Innate in each of us is the desire to have our lives count for what is important and lasting. We will put confidence in whatever we believe will lead to a life of significance. That's what you're doing right now. That's what I'm doing right now. Countless times in countless ways, every single day of our lives, our world is telling us to build our identity on the flesh and base our happiness in the flesh. The reference to *flesh* captures a way of living that is void of and in opposition to God. The world loves the allure of the flesh and as such it calls out to us, declaring that if we want to be happy and want to have a meaningful life, then we should live according to the flesh. It encourages us to live for the school that you went to, for how much money you can make, for who you marry, for what you look like, for what car you drive, for the clothes you wear. This is happening everywhere, and it is the reason many people have yet to find joy in this life. Friends, beware! This is a self-defeating strategy—if you live for your beauty, the day is coming where your beauty will fade. If you live for the muscles that you can build, the day is coming when your muscles begin to give way. Cars lose their shine and their smell. Money comes and goes. All of it is temporary, and if you are building your life on these things that please the flesh, then you are building your life on sand (Matt 7:24-26).

So, Paul warns the Philippians about those who will peddle a message that appeals to pleasing the flesh. He calls those who teach these things dogs, evildoers, and false circumcision (or mutilators of the flesh). They preached that in order to be made right with God, you needed to have faith in Jesus plus works, like upholding the Jewish law of circumcision. Paul vehemently opposes such a message. While these teachers have accused the Philippians of being unclean without circumcision, Paul says they (the false teachers) are the unclean scavengers, evildoers, and the real mutilators of the flesh, just like the pagans.

Friends, by way of reminder, it is for the sake of your joy that you be selective about those to whom you listen. Anyone who encourages you to trust in your ability to do anything that would make you right with God, they are deadly!

Paul helpfully applies the covenant sign of ethnic Israel to the church. He makes clear that the church is the true circumcision whose hearts have been circumcised with faith in Christ. Their glory is in Christ Jesus because they have no confidence in the flesh. Paul then leads into the example of his life, which has all the credentials that would be grounds for confidence in the flesh. This is the place he used to dig for the treasure of his worth. He begins with his pedigree—"circumcised on the eighth day, of the people of Israel, of the tribe of Benjamin, a Hebrew of Hebrews" (Phil 3:5). He then moves to his performance—"as to the law a Pharisee, as to zeal a persecutor of the church, as to righteousness under the law blameless" (Phil 3:6). Perhaps this resume does not strike you as impressive, but are you able to look past the particulars and identify how you too are prone to put confidence in the groups you belong to and/or the things you have done for right standing with the Lord? Are you aware of your own propensity to build your own resume? In what areas do you compare yourself with others in order to put confidence in the flesh? In what areas do you compare yourself with others only to be left defeated because you do not measure up? Paul says, "Do not put confidence in the flesh! Stop looking for validation that you can earn for yourself!" Paul does not just say, "Stop doing this;" he helpfully gives a better solution to find true joy and lasting validation.

"But whatever gain I had, I counted as loss for the sake of Christ" (Phil 3:7). Paul's language helps our mind's eye envision a ledger. Place every reason you have for confidence in the works of your flesh on one side of the ledger. Now place Christ on the other side. Paul believes that everything and anything that has been gained is loss when seen in view of Christ. To have everything while not having Jesus is to have nothing! To have nothing except Jesus while not having everything else is to have everything! Is Jesus this precious to you? What are you unwilling to lose, even if it means you gain Christ? Perhaps your desire to "gain the whole world" is the root of why you have so little joy and significance in this life. It just may be the reason "you forfeit your soul" (Mark 8:36). Non-Christian friends, gaining Christ will cost you every ounce of confidence that you can do anything to make yourself pleasing and acceptable in the sight of God. Christian brothers and sisters, you came to Christ having relinquished confidence in the flesh. You will get to glory doing the same.

Paul continues with the third encouragement.

3. Count Jesus far better than everything else (3:8-11)

The word *count* or *consider* that Paul uses in verses 8-9 means to give time for evaluation, to ponder. Here, Paul is encouraging these Christians to give time to consider Jesus Christ. Look back at the ledger: place all the gains in one column. Now place Jesus in the other column. All that once was gain is now loss. Not simply because they fail to be valuable but because they pale in comparison to the value that is found in him! Do not get lost in the math that Paul is doing here. Everything that you can think of when compared to Jesus is loss. Said another way: everything minus Jesus equals loss; nothing plus Jesus equals everything. This is the secret of having joy in all things. Paul has suffered the loss of everything and he's not mad. When we lose our keys, passwords, place in line, or assignments, we are prone to lose our cool as well as our joy! Paul has lost everything, and yet he knows joy. Is this how you think of the highs and the lows of life? Are we convinced that the good life is found when God is near to us, regardless of what is happening around us (Psalm 73:28)?

John Piper was once asked the question, "What is the greatest need of every missionary?" His response? "The greatest need of every missionary is to know Jesus better and to love Jesus more than anything else they know or love in all the world." The same is true for every college student, professor, faculty member, pastor, lawyer, stay-at-home mom, athlete, and student. In fact, this is the greatest need for every Christian. Jesus is worthy of such pursuit and allegiance because Jesus has no competitors. He is unrivaled. Until you see Jesus as supreme in all things and over all things, you have not seen him as he truly is. May we allow the Holy Spirit to search our hearts and reveal anything that needs to come into greater conformity to his will. How would you finish this sentence: I count everything as loss, as rubbish, as dung, compared to knowing Jesus, except for _____. Get that thing in your mind because as we are able to fill in that blank, we begin to identify what is competing for our joy and for a life that matters for the cause of God's glory. Oh friends, it is a deadly mistake to put our joy and our identity in anything as though it could provide what only Jesus can provide. Learn from Paul—no matter what life has thrown at him, his joy is secure and his hope persists because his treasure is Christ.

With Christ as his highest aim and most supreme satisfaction, Paul states he is willing to endure loss that he "may gain Christ" (Phil 3:8). He labors to ensure that these Philippian Christians know that faith, not works of the flesh, is the way to gain Christ. This is what it means to be a follower of Jesus. Christians cannot satisfy the righteous requirements of God's law by what they do. The righteousness Paul speaks of is not an issue of moral integrity but moral perfection. Any and all who would follow Christ must turn from their inability to attain perfection and receive, through faith, the perfection of Jesus Christ. To gain Christ is to turn from the sin that keeps us from loving and obeying God as we ought, and to believe in the sinless life, in the substitutionary death, in the bodily resurrection of Jesus Christ from the grave for the forgiveness of our sins. Repentance from sin and faith in this message is our only hope to gain Christ.

Non-Christian friend, I would plead with you today to bring your parched souls to the fountain of living water that is Jesus Christ. Come to him with hands that have clung to the things of this world and find acceptance, love, mercy, and forgiveness when you empty your hands and lay hold of him. It will cost you everything and yet when you gain Christ, you will realize you've lost nothing. He is unmatched in his sufficiency. There is more mercy in him than sin in you, so turn from sin and trust in him. Who else holds out this kind of joy to you? Coming to Christ is not the end of joy as you've known it. Rather, it is the beginning of joy that you have always longed for, never have to be ashamed of, and that can never be taken away from you. Come to Jesus.

When we trust in him, God declares us righteous. Christian, there is no need to cower in fear as though something else will be brought up to testify against you and so sway God to change his mind. You will fail and miss the mark, but your righteousness does not rest on your ability to hold on to God. It rests in his ability to hold fast until the end. It rests in the righteousness of Christ that has been credited to all who repent and believe. Christians, live in this! God is not a God who's got a buzzer in hand, waiting on us to fail just to condemn us again. He has given us lasting joy in Christ. Paul feasts on the full hope of the gospel as he mentions the life, death, and resurrection of Christ. If gaining Christ means sharing in suffering, Paul readily accepts suffering. It is attractive to want to gain Christ by means of his victories, but Paul wants to know him through the fellowship of his sufferings. Consider the sufferings of Jesus—he did not revile, he did not curse, he entrusted himself to the care of his Father. We too will learn how to delight more in him as well as how to better respond to him through the fellowship we share with him in suffering. Suffering can be endured because power has been supplied. Paul wants to know the power of his resurrection, which is power that courses through the life of every Christian. Paul wants to live in conscious dependence on that power. When life is over, he knows that the power of his resurrection will give way then to the presence of the resurrection. This is the secret to his joy—to know, gain, and possess Jesus in the resurrection. A reality of no more death, no more suffering, fullness of joy, and pleasures forevermore. A place where tears will be wiped away from the eyes, saints eating at the marriage supper of the Lamb. A future where no temple is needed because the Lamb is the temple, where no sun needed because the glory of the slain Lamb is the light. An eternity of all of us looking away from ourselves and looking unto Jesus. The experience of your joy is directly connected to how precious Jesus is to you. If Jesus is not precious to you, then do not be surprised that you lack joy and satisfaction that comes through a life lived for him.

4. Press on towards the prize of Christ (3:12-16)

Followers of Jesus don't drift towards godliness; they strain and press forward. There is a hunger that awakens when one is made right with God. We do not live on past accomplishments or even past intimacy with the Lord. We do not move on from the gospel. We revel in the work of Christ and that reveling compels us stay the course of the gospel. Christian brothers and sisters, stay the course of the gospel. It is the common practice for followers of Jesus who have gained Christ to humbly acknowledge that they haven't arrived and to passionately pursue a greater knowledge of the Savior. May we prayerfully lean into this sort of gospel humility that will help us see ourselves accurately as well as inform how gracious we are with others who are just as much works in progress as we are. May we also, motivated by grace, seek to make necessary changes to our lives that we may know God more truly and enjoy him more fully. By looking unto Jesus, followers of Jesus position themselves not to lose the wonder of the gospel. That look unto Christ is how Christians press on towards the goal for the prize of the upward call in Christ Jesus. Gospel-centered humility informing gospel-motivated effort is instrumental in walking honorably before the Lord.

Lastly, the fifth encouragement.

5. Follow other cross-bearing disciples until glory (3:17-21)

These encouragements seem daunting when we consider our limitations and struggles. But God did not design for his people to walk in these ways on their own. This pursuit of joy and purpose is not a solo endeavor for the Christian who is sufficient in these things. No, this life is one whereby other Christians need us, and we need them. The God-ordained venue for such a Christ-treasuring and Christ-enjoying life is the context of a faithful local church. We are helpers and keepers of one another until glory, whereby we receive from Christ the bodies that will be suitable and sufficient for an eternity of joy. Christian friends, who are you imitating that is helping you know the Lord more truly and experience his joy more fully? Is your example worth commending to others towards the same ends?

Conclusion

These five encouragements are written that the Philippians would experience joy and meaningful living to the fullest. When we too come to the Christ that Paul commends here in Philippians 3, we too are invited into such joy and fullness of life. Many scholars and teachers view this chapter as Paul writing his epitaph. If we could summarize all of his life into a few words for a tombstone, what would it say? While there is benefit in considering the end of our days, I do think that living for a few words on stone leaves something to be desired. Words will fade, stones will crumble, so I call us to stop trying to make a name for ourselves but rather take his name as our own. Live for Christ! Gain Christ! Be willing to lose it all for Christ! May we not waste our lives trying to run a race to nowhere that no one will remember. Joy cannot be found in that life, and significance is not known this way. Rejoice in the Lord! Put no confidence in your flesh! Consider Jesus far better than everything else! Press on toward the prize of Christ! Follow other cross-bearing disciples to glory!

Chapter 6

THE CHURCH AND
THE CHRIST-LIFE

Philippians 4:1-9

Phil Newton[1]

Introduction

If you open your Bibles this morning to Philippians 4, we're going to look at what may be a familiar passage. You know, some of those easy memory verses: "Rejoice in the Lord always; again, I'll say rejoice." But let's begin in verse 1, and we'll look at verses 1-9. Now, I want us to think about inside the Christian Church, the church and the Christ-life.

Hear God's Word:

> Therefore, my brothers, whom I love and long for, my joy and crown, stand firm thus in the Lord, my beloved.
>
> I entreat Euodia and I entreat Syntyche to agree in the Lord. Yes, I ask you also, true companion, help these women, who have labored side by side with me in the gospel together with Clement and the rest of my fellow workers, whose names are in the book of life.
>
> Rejoice in the Lord always; again, I will say rejoice. Let your reasonableness be known to everyone. The Lord is at hand; do not be anxious about anything, but in everything by prayer and supplication with thanksgiving let your requests be made

---

[1] Phil Newton is Director of Pastoral Care and Mentoring for the Pillar Network.

known to God. And the peace of God, which surpasses all understanding, will guard your hearts and your minds in Christ Jesus.

Finally, brothers, whatever is true, whatever is honorable, whatever is just, whatever is pure, whatever is lovely, whatever is commendable, if there is any excellence, if there is anything worthy of praise, think about these things. What you have learned and received and heard and seen in me—practice these things, and the God of peace will be with you.

This is God's Word. May he write that Word on our hearts.

Well, I began my first staff position over fifty years ago as a college student, preparing for vocational ministry. And it should have been obvious that the church did not know what they were doing. They asked me to be their music minister (they probably called it music *director*). Maybe they should have taken music off and just said director. And just to tell you how bad it was, I had to ask my roommate for a crash course in 4/4 timing before I went to the church. So, I didn't know anything about leading music, but I agreed to do it if they would let me work with the youth. And so, here I was in this church that had all kinds of issues going on. I didn't know what a healthy church was supposed to look like. I don't know that I'd ever given a lot of thought to it. I just had this church position so that I could teach these teenagers while somewhat nervously trying to lead an erstwhile choir and the congregation in singing. I think I learned more of what *not* to do in church by being there than I learned what to do. The pastor was disengaged. The congregation was highly divided, and the atmosphere was toxic. And it was many, many years later before I was part of a church that really seemed healthy. And then it took me more time to learn that even in healthy churches, you still have issues. You still face difficulties, and you have to be regularly reminded of the practices that leave the church looking more like Jesus, because that's what he wants us to look like.

And that's where I think we find Paul with the Philippian church. They were dear to his heart. They were gospel partners. They were a joy to him. They were regularly in his prayers. They were a church that had great concern for his welfare. And while we find a few issues along the way that maybe needed to be addressed, nothing grabs you like the Corinthian divisiveness or the Galatian legalism. Overall, the Philippian church modeled what it looked like to be a healthy church. And yet, a healthy church doesn't mean that you've arrived. It doesn't mean that everything is just right, any more than Paul thought he had arrived. Even healthy churches need exhortations to persevere, to correct weak areas, and to grow in living the Christ-life.

And here's what I want to press upon us in this text—that *local churches must learn to corporately live the Christ-life.* It's something we do together. And if the Philippian church was overall an admirably healthy church, then what did they need to concentrate on to grow in spiritual health and to manifest Christ's life in the community? There's a series of exhortations here—seven of them—that move the church toward a healthy life in Christ. And I want us to think about those together.

The first one is this: hold your ground.

1. Hold your ground (4:1)

He begins, "Therefore, my brothers . . ." So, he's tying this text to the previous section (3:17-21), where Paul has exhorted the church to imitate him and those who are living the Christ-life. He warns of enemies of the cross. He reminds believers that they have a citizenship in heaven. And then he says, "Therefore, my brothers, whom I love and long for, my joy and crown, stand firm, thus in the Lord, my beloved" (4:1). So, he reiterates his love for them, his longing for them, his present joy in seeing

Christ being formed in them, and that sense of future joy and reward as the Philippian church serves as a crown to him when he stands before the Lord.

And yet, he still exhorts them. I mean, I would love compliments like this, wouldn't you? And yet, he exhorts them that they had not arrived. The church that gets comfortable and complacent puts itself in a dangerous spot. Instead, he says, "Stand firm in the Lord." This is an idea of firmness, of uprightness. It was a word that was used when someone stood in the Roman amphitheater with all the odds stacked against him, and he was to hold his ground. And brothers and sisters, that's what we must do.

What does that imply when we hold our ground doctrinally and we hold our ground in practice? Now, Paul used the same word earlier in 1:27-28, "Only let your manner of life be worthy of the gospel of Christ, so that whether I come and see you or am absent, I may hear of you that you are standing firm in one spirit with one mind, striving side by side for the faith of the gospel and not frightened by anything by your opponents." One stands firmly on the good news of the crucified and resurrected Savior, who graciously saves sinners and reigns as Lord. And as we stand together in one spirit, we have united minds, and we have united hearts in the beauty and power of the gospel.

Now, I would submit to you that it's not hard to get people to stand together for a project or in a church for building a building, or maybe joining and following a charismatic person's vision for the church. But it is quite a different thing to stand together so that the gospel of Jesus Christ informs and motivates and shapes our practices. I ran into this years ago. In one church I pastored, we had rallied together in planting a church and building a building, and everything seemed like it was going great. But when the construction was finished and we began to look at ourselves, we didn't have anything holding us together. We lacked the gospel as the solid foundation upon which we built our lives. And things unraveled.

Hold your ground. Hold your ground by standing and living in the gospel of Jesus. Second, treasure your unity.

2. Treasure your unity (4:2-3)

Verses 2-3 may be the most awkward in this epistle. Paul identifies—he calls out—two ladies who are at odds with each other. Some suggest that they held an office or leadership role (maybe there were deaconesses in the church). But publicly, without shaming them or without belittling them, Paul identifies an issue that was so serious it deserves space in this letter. And so, he writes, "I entreat Euodia and I entreat Syntyche to agree in the Lord" (4:2). Now, Paul doesn't identify the problem, but whatever it was, it was divisive enough that the church sought Paul's counsel in trying to get it resolved. And his gracious approach, and his call for help in relieving the tensions, is really a model for healthy congregationalism.

In the first church that I pastored (many years ago), there were 40 in attendance, rain or shine, all days—except when they had cemetery decorations. Some of you don't know what that is. Ask your grandparents; they will tell you. And I didn't realize until six months into the pastorate that two of the ladies in the church were sisters. They never had anything to do with each other. I found out much later that one of them had made an off-handed comment to the other. And that one took offense. And there were years and years they didn't speak. They were in the same church, always sat on opposite sides, never had anything to do with each other until one of them almost died. And then, by God's grace, they reconciled; they restored peace. But what these ladies maybe didn't realize at the time was that their disunity hindered the unity of that small congregation. I mean, I saw it creeping in the church business meetings in which one family always took the opposite side of the other family. I mean, with 40 people, you add those two that are at odds and their families at odds, and that was a pretty high percentage. So, I ask, "Do we treasure the unity that we have in

Christ?" (or what Paul calls "to agree in the Lord").

It's a word that implies that we are agreeing in attitude. We are agreeing in disposition that we have toward one another because those attitudes and dispositions have been shaped by the cross of Christ. It is the spirit of forgiveness and humility for the sake of the gospel that calls us to lay aside our petty differences. Paul thought this unity of attitude and disposition so important that he addresses it. He presses it on this Philippian church.

Now, do we put as much weight on that as Paul did? Couldn't the church just let it go? Well, Paul didn't think so. And in what one New Testament scholar (Moisés Silva) calls "a striking emphasis . . . on corporate responsibility . . ." that "reaches a dramatic high point in the exhortation when you get to verse three," Paul calls for action. He says in verse 3, "Yes, I ask you also, true companion, help these women, who have labored side by side with me in the gospel together with Clement and the rest of my fellow workers, whose names are in the book of life." Now, we don't know who the true companion is. I think a good case can be made for Luke, because Paul evidently left him in Philippi when he had to "get out of Dodge" in a hurry with all that was going on. You can see that in Acts 16:17. You don't see Luke mentioned again. You don't see any more "we" passages until you get to Acts 20:5, when Paul is again swinging through Macedonia, this area of Philippi. And we don't know who Clement is. He may have been the pastor, or he could have been the husband of one of these women. But if it was Luke that Paul called upon, he was not to let disunity fester in the church, but he was to humbly (not with a club, but humbly) bring these women together to see the weight of their disagreement—that it smacked of pride and self-importance, and it hampered the treasure of the church's unity. But he was not to treat them as troublemakers. He was not to treat them as agitators or spiritual failures. Their names were written in the Lamb's book of life. They were counted as faithful followers of Christ. They stood by Paul in laboring in the gospel.

These were solid Christians, but they got off track. And so, what did they need? They needed someone else to come alongside. They needed the church to come alongside and point out the burr under their saddle so that they would get the burr out from under their saddle and be able to move forward and live in graciousness. Do we do our part as church members to be, as Paul put it earlier in Philippians 2, "of the same mind, having the same love, being in full accord and of one mind, to do nothing from selfish ambition or conceit, but in humility, count others more significant than ourselves" (2:2-3)? We treasure the church's unity together through humble dispositions, through a consciousness of our partnership in the gospel, and by keeping an eternal perspective together that our names are written in the book of life.

Third, maintain your joy.

3. Maintain your joy (4:4)

"Rejoice in the Lord always; again, I will say rejoice" (4:4). The great Welsh preacher of the last century, Martin Lloyd-Jones, remarked, "Nothing is more characteristic of the life of the first Christians than this element of joy." And in these final exhortations, Paul just continues this theme of joy that you've been hearing about during the expositions of Philippians. And so, think about it. He's sitting in a Roman prison. He didn't have a color television set and access to the golf course. I mean, this was a hard time. And yet, he modeled joy. And so, he was qualified to exhort these Christians living under persecution to maintain joy in the Lord.

I love what Ulrich Zwingli, the Swiss reformer, said and how he described it. He said, "It is such the mark of the Christian mind to always be rejoicing, always cheerful, even in the midst of tribulations with a thousand adversaries." Even when they threaten, we are to have this kind of joy. But this joy is not a plastic smile that turns upward when we're around Christians or we come to chapel, and then when we're away, it just drops to the ground. See, this joy has been developed in our hearts by relationship to Christ. We go deep in that well of life in Jesus, and he fills us to the point that that joy is contagious.

Let me give you four aspects of it. ***First, rejoicing is intentional.*** By intentionality, we're letting the rich truths of the gospel, and the fruit of the gospel, cause us to praise the Lord. We were singing about that a moment ago. How does that happen? By our meditations upon Christ—bearing our sins on the cross, being raised from the dead, those promises in the gospel that never end—informing our minds and our dispositions about whatever the circumstances may be. ***Second, rejoicing is experiential.*** Rejoicing is about relationship with Christ. I mean, what is there not to be thankful for if you're a sinner saved by grace? There are only two reasons we don't have joy. One is we do not know Christ and his saving power. Two, we've gotten distracted and focused on ourselves, and we've lost our vision of setting our affections upon Christ. Cultivate relationship with Jesus to cultivate joy. ***Third, rejoicing is expansive.*** And by that, I mean joy in Jesus covers the whole of life, the whole of our circumstances, which is why Zwingli mentioned a thousand adversaries threatening discouragement and destructions not being enough to stall our joy when we're fixed upon Jesus Christ. Now, if you're having trouble in this area, let me suggest something. Get your Bible out, and start reading the four Gospels. And when you finish them, go back and reread them. And when you see Jesus and his life and you see his love and you see him going to the cross and suffering in your place and rising from the dead and ascending to the Father, you'll get on with joy because it's found in him. Learn to rejoice when things are sweet and agreeable, because I assure you that times will come where things are bitter and difficult. And if you've not been stoking and storing your heart with joy in those agreeable times, you're going to be sunk when you get to those bitter times. Prepare now. Live in joy by learning daily to set your affections on Christ. ***And then fourth, rejoicing is forward-looking.*** I mean, we've read of when we see Jesus face-to-face and he wipes every tear from our eyes and there's no more sin and suffering and death. We've read of our names in the Lamb's book of life. I mean, I hope you've read through the book of Revelation and you've seen that it is a book of worship and joy, because that's where the Lord is taking us forever.

Number four, remember your kindliness.

4. Remember your kindliness (4:5)

Now, I picked that word because I think it picks up the idea of what Paul means in verse 5: "Let your reasonableness"—let your moderation, as the New American Standard translates it—"be known to everyone. The Lord is near." We can translate it: "Let your general attitude be known to all men, or let your sweet reasonableness be known to all men." Here's a sense, as one Greek scholar put it, of "a humble, patient, steadfastness, which is able to submit to injustice and disgrace and maltreatment without hate and malice" because the person is trusting in the Lord (see Cleon Rogers Jr. and Cleon Rogers, III). Bishop Lightfoot calls it "the opposite of a spirit of contention and self-seeking." Maybe the best way to put it is that this reasonableness or this kindliness looks like Jesus. Again, Lloyd-Jones calls it "one of the highest demands of the Christian gospel" because we are asked to be like Jesus.

And yet, is this not what the Holy Spirit does in the fruit of the Spirit? Is he not reproducing in us the character of the Lord Jesus Christ? I mean, think about particularly patience, kindness, goodness, gentleness. That's not something that we manufacture. You don't grab a book and read it and say, "I'm going to follow the instructions and get this." This is the life of Christ in you. And this spirit of kindliness is to be manifested through us.

But why don't we see more of it among those who profess to be followers of Christ? Some people have no power for it because Christ is not in them. And if that's the case in your life, I point you to Jesus who changes everything, who will turn you upside down and inside out. For others, if we would show kindness—the kindness of Jesus—we must live in Jesus. When we grow in the grace and knowledge of Christ, we are living in him. When we put on Christ and make no provision for the flesh to obey its desires, we're living in him. When we die to sin and live to righteousness, we're living in him. Live *in him*, so that you might be *like him*. But Jesus made provision for this. Peter says, "He himself bore our sins in his body on the tree, in order that we might die to sin and live to righteousness. By his wounds, you've been healed" (1 Peter 2:23-24). And so, our great Shepherd and Overseer, the Lord Jesus, has put his life in us in regeneration. And he's given us power in him to kill sin and live his righteous life.

And then Paul adds, "The Lord is at hand." Keep that in mind. Let that affect the way that you focus on living this kind of kindliness of life.

Number five, persist in prayer.

5. Persist in prayer (4:6-7)

You say, "Of course, we need to pray. That's just part of being a Christian, isn't it? It's basic." And yet, do we pray instead of fretting and complaining? Do we pray as a first line of action? Or do we wait until we've exhausted all of our abilities, and then we pray? Do we pray as the work foundational to all other work or merely a help to get us to the real work? Now, this well-known passage helps us. "Do not be anxious about anything, but in everything by prayer and supplication with thanksgiving let your requests be made known to God. And the peace of God, which surpasses all understanding, will guard your hearts and minds in Christ Jesus" (4:6-7).

One old writer put it, "Anxiety and prayer are more opposed to each other than fire and water." You see, our hearts tend to feel the weight of troubles. Things don't go as we hoped. People turn against us, carefully laid plans fall through, the job we knew was going to happen doesn't, that potential spouse drops you. Anxiety strikes. But prayer turns anxiety to the Lord God. Prayer recognizes the wise, sovereign working of the Lord as he unfolds his purposes for us. Prayer entrusts our burdens to the Lord.

When I was a junior in college, our ministerial group—there were, I don't know, 40 or 50 of us—went to Birmingham and Dr. Stephen Olford was preaching—a great British expositor. And he spoke just to our group of college students. And I remember him preaching on one verse from Psalm 37: "Commit your way to the Lord; trust in him and he will act" (Psalm 37:5). And I can still hear him rolling his r's, translating that verse as "roll your way onto the Lord." And it struck me; it's affected me for 50 years, in thinking about that, that when there's a burden too heavy to lift, just roll it. You can't always lift those things; roll it onto the Lord. We give it to him.

And Paul uses multiple terms to express his prayer: supplication, requests made known to God, and all with thanksgiving, because to pray without thanksgiving, as one writer put it, is to clip the wings of prayer. Because in thanksgiving, you are acknowledging the wisdom, goodness, and grace of the Lord. You're acknowledging the wisdom of his providence at work, governing your life. You're expressing your trust and confidence that he is sufficient and faithful. And it confesses that he's the source of all blessing.

Now, the Philippians were accustomed to seeing Roman sentries standing as a garrison, guarding them and keeping them secure. And so, Paul flips this idea and says, "And the peace of God"—you're praying, you're rolling these burdens on the Lord, you're entrusting them to him—"and the peace of God, which surpasses all understanding will guard your hearts"—garrison your hearts, be a sentinel to your hearts "and your minds in Christ Jesus." I mean, anxiety troubles us, but what prayer does is it rolls those anxious deeds onto the Lord

and it brings that peace of the Lord. That doesn't mean you flip a switch and say, "I got it. Okay, I'm praying; here it is." No, you're probably going to have to wrestle with some of those anxious thoughts. You're going to have to go to the Word as you go to the Lord in prayer. You're going to have to think upon him. And as you do, the peace of God begins to affect you.

It is the peace of God because he is a God of peace. He gives you himself. It is the peace which God gives, which has been given to us in the Lord Jesus Christ. And he's calling for this to happen for the whole church, that we are to be seeking him in prayer. I mean, think about those believers living under persecution. They were to roll their burdens onto the Lord, and the peace of God would affect them. He sweeps over us as the divine sentinel of the heart and mind.

Number six, guard your thinking.

6. Guard your thinking (4:8)

Now, to guard our thinking means we guard our hearts, and to guard our hearts means we guard our walks. For Jesus declared, "But what comes out of the mouth proceeds from the heart, and this defiles a person" (Matt 15:18). And so, what Paul does is he lays out a plan for the heart and the mind that cultivates healthy meditations upon the Lord. And these are corporate practices that he's speaking of. How does the body live out the Christ-life together? Well, it's a call to encourage one another, to model godliness for one another, and to be ready to humbly nudge one another along this path of life that looks like Christ. And so, you'll notice what he says in verse 8: "Finally, brothers, whatever is true, whatever is honorable, whatever is just, whatever is pure, whatever is lovely, whatever is commendable, if there is any excellence, if there is anything worthy of praise, think about these things." That last phrase is literally, "Take into account these things." And so, what he's doing is he's calling for meditating on and thinking on to the point that these things shape your lives as a gathered body of believers. In other words, he's not giving us so much of a checklist by which we filter our thoughts as much as he's giving us a template for remembering God's goodness in our lives through Christ, so that these things affect the way that we live. I mean, think about it. What might be true, honorable, just, pure, lovely, and commendable more than Jesus Christ? More than his faithful redemptive work and promises? Lloyd-Jones rightly puts it, "The New Testament never asks us to contemplate ideas. It always calls upon us to look at the Person." Another writer points out that Paul exhorts us to embrace the best of what God is doing now and will do for eternity, as long as it is understood in the light of the cross [Gordon Fee]. And so, in these things, we're called to be controlled in our thinking and actions by the person of Jesus and his work in the gospel.

Number seven, follow good models.

7. Follow good models (4:9)

"What you have learned and received and heard and seen in me— practice these things, and the God of peace will be with you" (4:9). The Christian life cannot—cannot!—be lived passively, which means, as the local gathered body of believers, we can't be passive about what we believe or how we think or how we live. And this is the problem in many church circles. We're just programmed to kind of check the boxes. Okay, I've shown up, I've attended service, I've participated in a few events, I've given a little money, and I'm not complaining about anything. Instead, we are to be a people who love the gospel together to the point that its powerful truths are affecting the way we believe and think and behave. We're concerned with living the Christ-life. We're not to substitute a sterile, religious observance for the passion of living daily in Christ and his gospel.

And this is where Paul had no hesitation, when he said, "Brothers and sisters, what you've learned from me on your path as disciples, what you've received from my teaching, what you've heard in the way I speak to others and you've seen in the way I treat others in walking with Jesus, just do these things." Just do it. Practice these things. Live life in Christ. Pay attention to your walks. Be serious about your obedience, your disciplining yourself for the purpose of godliness, being holy as the Lord is holy. Follow good examples that help you toward that end.

Conclusion

There's a sense that this passage comes full circle. Stand firm in the Lord and practice life in Christ by following those who set faithful examples of living as Christians. The entire passage considers how the church practices the Christ-life. It's found in how we stand in the gospel. It's found in how we treasure unity, and how we maintain joy in Christ, and how we remember to be like Jesus in kindness, and how we persist in prayer, and how we guard our thinking, and how we follow models of those who live for the Christ life. What happens when the Lord so works in us that these things become evident? Well, Paul says, "Practice these things, and the God of peace will be with you" (4:9).

Chapter 7

THE SECRET OF CONTENTMENT

Philippians 4:10-20

Ray Van Neste[1]

Introduction

Are you content? You might ask, "What do you mean by that?" We don't use that word a whole lot today.[2] Are you satisfied? Again, you might say, "Well, I'm not satisfied with where I am. I want to grow. I want to develop. I want to become more. That's why I'm here at college." That's why some of you are here visiting and trying to seek God's will concerning where you should go to college. And, yes, you want to press on, you want to grow. What I'm referring to isn't opposed to that, but I'm asking, "Do you have a deep satisfaction down in your soul, so that even as you seek to grow, even as you want to accomplish things and to have an impact, you know if all those things fall apart everything's still okay?" Or are you aiming at and desiring many things, because really down deep in your soul, you are trying your best to prove that you matter? Maybe to convince others, maybe to convince yourself that you have value, that you're important, that you're okay? I think that's where many of us are. But if you're there, you know how terrible it is to be in that place.

If you need one more thing to prove that you're OK, and then if one

---

[1] Ray Van Neste is Vice President for University Ministries and Dean of the School of Theology and Missions at Union University.

[2] Perry Glanzer wrote about contentment in "One of the Most Understudied Virtues is also One We Desperately Need," Christian Scholars blog, April 12, 2024. He even details how the word itself has received declining amount of attention in print. https://christianscholars.com/one-of-the-most-understudied-virtues-is-also-one-we-desperately-need-2/ .

of those things falls apart, it can shatter you. It challenges your identity, your value, and your purpose. And, all of a sudden, it feels like everything has fallen apart. This is why people's disapproval of us has such a large impact. You might hear people saying that you shouldn't be worried, and you shouldn't be so fragile, but you think, "Sure, I shouldn't, but this is where I am."

This, I think, is what's behind what a number of analysts are beginning to call an epidemic of unhappiness in our culture.[3] This deep-seated unhappiness, despite all the comforts and opportunities we have, is due to our lack of this deep, settled contentment. Such contentment is what the Scriptures promise us.

In Philippians 4:10-13, Paul says he has learned the secret of contentment. If we think carefully about what I just described, I think we want to know what this secret is. And in fact, "secret" is kind of a weird word from Paul to use here since in various other places he's at pains to make sure we know that there isn't secret knowledge for select people in the church. But here he knows a secret, and he wants to share it with us.

In this text Paul is wrapping up what he's been saying throughout the letter of Philippians. You can tell Paul is wanting to say thank you, but he's being very careful about it. He might sound like somebody in your life whom you have helped, who stammers about trying to tell you thank you, and you think, "Just say it!"

In verse 10 Paul acknowledges that they have helped him, and then seems to hurry in verse 11 to say, "Not that I'm speaking of being in need." It sounds like he's saying, thank you for giving to me, not that I needed anything. But, that's not really what he's doing. Instead, he's being careful

---

[3] "Something is wrong. Throughout the West, people are angry, anxious, and discontented. Paradoxically, the ill temper arises amid wealth unimaginable to our recent ancestors. ... Shouldn't we be at ease, sated or at least palliated by material and technical advances that have taken so much suffering out of life?", "Everyday Freedom," R. R. Reno, *First Things* (April 2024) 342: 63.

not to undercut the things he's been saying through this letter about contentment. He's saying, there was a lack and you went out of your way to help me with it and I'm so grateful for it, but I just want you to know I was content in the Lord even in the lack.

In fact, as we go through this text, his great celebration isn't even so much about what he received but the grace demonstrated in the lives of the people who helped him. He's far more excited to say, "Wow, look what God is doing in you since you were willing to give!" He's far more interested in that than meeting his own needs.

Verses 11-12 state the same basic point three ways, piling up emphasis.[4]

v.11	I have learned		in whatever situation
v.12a	I know I know		brought low abound
v.12b	I have learned	secret	facing plenty & hunger, abundance & nee

This repetition stresses that Paul has learned and come to know how to be content in any situation, good or bad. That's why he said, thank you, but I'm most pleased to see what God's doing in your life because I've learned in all of these settings to be content.

We probably know we should be content in every situation, but do we really live that way? Are we more content or more happy when all the things are going our way? We probably are. And, don't hear me wrong. I'm not saying next time everything's going your way make sure you get mad a little bit. Rather, the Scriptures are pushing us to ask, "What is the foundation of our joy? Is it that things are going well? Is it that you have what you want? Or is it something deeper?" You've learned in life to this

---

[4] Throughout this sermon I am referring to the ESV for the biblical text.

point that things go well sometimes, and they go poorly sometimes. And if your contentment and your joy is based on the circumstances then your joy is going to come and go. You, and those around you, will experience emotional whiplash as you swing back and forth.

In fact, I think we tend to look for our contentment in comfort, consumption, and credit.

Comfort. If I can have what makes me feel good, then I'm happy. And the Bible is all for comfort in its right setting. It's a great gift, but a terrible god. If you make that your pursuit, then when you get it, if you accomplish that often, it's just going to lead to you being soft and unable to face difficult things.

Consumption. If I can gain or consume more and more things, that will make me happy. God encourages us to enjoy the good things that come our way, but excess is a problem. And, if consumption becomes your goal and you succeed in accumulating more and more, it will just make you conceited and self-centered.

Credit. If I am recognized and celebrated enough for what you do, then I will be satisfied. Again, this is a good thing done rightly: "honor to whom honor is owed" (Rom 13:7). But if you live for recognition and succeed in getting a good bit of it, that will just make you an arrogant jerk, seeking and demanding everybody else's attention.

Furthermore, in all of these, when those become our goal, we can't rejoice in other people getting those things because we want them coming to us. Here is one way to gauge your heart. When you hear somebody, maybe a friend, maybe an enemy, getting some credit, getting a comfortable situation, getting some of the things they want, things going really well for them— when you hear that, can you fully and freely rejoice in what has come to them? That's what we should do. But when we find ourselves thinking, "I wanted that!", something is exposed in our hearts.

So, Paul says here in verse 11, he has learned in whatever situation to be content. He's learned this. He wasn't born this way just like we weren't. He has learned this in the school of Christ. This is part of discipleship. He says, "I know how to be brought low. I know how to abound. In every circumstance I have learned the secret of facing plenty and hunger, abundance, and need."

It does not, though, tell us here what the secret is. Paul is looking to that whole line of thought about joy, which he has developed in this letter. We will need to trace that theme to clarify the "secret."

But let me first deal with a common misconception about verse 13. Verse 13 is one of those verses that gets pulled out of context and put in all kinds of places. "I can do all things through him who strengthens me." You may have seen the little cartoon where a wife asks her husband to open a jar and he's doing his best to twist it open as he quotes, "I can do all things through Christ who strengthens me." The wife says, "Honey, twist the jar, not the Scriptures." Paul is not saying you can quote this verse and pass your test without studying. He's not saying you can box and expect to win. This is not a promise of success in every endeavor. He is saying, "I have learned how to be content even when everything falls apart."

We live in a fallen world, and sometimes terrible things happen. There is great sorrow and suffering in the world. Some of you know this by experience. When Paul talks about contentment, he does not mean something glib, just telling you to put a smile on your face anyway. The point is not to go around singing, "Everything is awesome," when it's not. Paul is saying that he can be content even in very difficult situations because Christ will empower him. It takes real power to be content, and Christ will strengthen you to enable you to be content in the worst of times.

Now, contentment is the foundation for joy. So, this theme of joy that runs through this letter is what he is pointing back to. Let's look back to key texts where this theme arises previously in the letter.

In 1:12 we begin to see this when he says, "I want you to know brothers that what has happened to me," and what has happened to him is being thrown in prison. Prison in the first century was a very bad place. Nothing plush about it. People often never got over the damage prison did to their health, and many died due to imprisonment. So, Paul in a terrible, life-threatening, tough place says, "I want you to know that what has happened to me has really served to advance the gospel so that it has become known throughout the whole Imperial Guard and to all the rest that my imprisonment is for Christ" (1:12-13).

So, what's he saying? He's in prison so he has no earthly comfort. And he says, "Hey, I know you may be worried about me since you've heard that I'm in prison. I just want to tell you it's amazing! Not the accommodations, but the accomplishment of the gospel. God has put me here. I wanted to preach the gospel in Rome, and now I'm here and the whole Imperial Guard has heard it! This is a great day."

Now we might read that and think, "So, he was crazy." No. But you can begin to see what his chief aim in life was. It wasn't his comfort. But it was the advance of the gospel. You see, what determines whether or not we can be content with certain things is what you are after. If we're after our comfort, it's not going to work. If we're after Christ's exaltation, then that is going to happen one way or another. Then, what we are pursuing, what we have our hearts set on, is assured to happen.

But he goes on, saying in 1:14, "And most of the brothers, having become confident in the Lord by my imprisonment, are much more bold to speak the word without fear." That's a good thing! "Some indeed preach Christ from envy and rivalry, but others from good will. The latter do it out of love, knowing that I put him for the defense of the gospel. The former proclaim Christ out of selfish ambition, not sincerely but thinking to afflict me in my imprisonment. What then? Only that in every way, whether in pretense or in truth, Christ is proclaimed, and in that I rejoice" (1:15-18).

What's he saying? He's saying, "I'm excited about being in prison because this has made more people bold to preach the gospel. And okay, all right, you've heard so you know, so I'll put it on the table. I know some people are preaching Christ so as to give me a hard time. Some people are trying to steal credit from me." If Paul was living for credit, then he'd be ticked off and frustrated. But since he's living for Christ to be exalted, he says, "You boys go for it! So what about my credit! Christ is being preached."

Hey Paul, people aren't hearing about you so much because you're in prison. Your name's kind of fading. And these other people are better known as preachers of the Gospel. Paul says, "Are they preaching the true Gospel? They are? Then I'm perfectly fine with it." *This* is the path to contentment, and it leads to joy.

Now if you keep going in chapter 1, you get to verses 20-23 in which we find this striking statement, "For me to live is Christ and to die is gain" (1:21). What's he getting at? Well, he has just said, "My eager expectation . . . [is that] Christ will be honored in my body whether by life or by death" (1:20). And in fact, if I live, it's Christ living. If I die, it's gain because I go to be with him. What's his aim? Christ. So even the threat of death does not destroy his joy, does not shake his contentment. He's in prison, he's eventually going to be executed. You could imagine somebody even saying to him, "Paul, I see what you're writing there to the Philippians, what if the word came right now that they were going to take you away and chop your head off? Are you still gonna be so joyful?" His answer in the text is, "Yes!" Again, I think some folks would think he's crazy. Why are you joyful? "Because the worst thing you can do to me is send me to the Jesus whom I serve, whom I love, for whom my life is given; the worst thing you can do is give me a ticket to his presence. Bring it on!" This is solid joy.

He picks this theme up again over at 2:5-11, that great text where he tells us to have the mindset of Jesus. Philippians 2:5–8: "Have this mind among yourselves, which is yours in Christ Jesus, who, though he was in the form of God, did not count equality with God a thing to be grasped, but emptied himself, by taking the form of a servant, being born in the likeness of men. And being found in human form, he humbled himself by becoming obedient to the point of death, even death on a cross."

Notice this mindset of Jesus. It is not stuck on his comfort, his consumption, or even his credit. He gave it all up. He left his place in glory. He took on suffering, even to the point of the most horrendous death that was known. He did all that. And what did he get it? Well, finish that paragraph. "Therefore, God has highly exalted him and bestowed on him the name that is above every name, so that at the name of Jesus every knee should bow, in heaven and on earth and under the earth, and every tongue confess that Jesus Christ is Lord, to the glory of God the Father" (2:9-11).

He gave it all up and got it all back! In the gospel paradigm, the way up is down. And he's not just telling us this is what Jesus did. He says, "Have this mind in you!" Recognize that the way of the cross is to lay your life down and trust the Lord that he will give you back far more than you could ever give up.

If we know that, there is contentment. Somebody says, sinfulness around us has harmed us or taken things away, or simply a fallen world that brought things to bear on our lives that are hard, difficult, or even evil. We don't rejoice in those things, but we rejoice in the God who is sovereign over all things and still has us in his hand and will not allow anything to come into our lives except that which he will use for our own good.

See, there is another challenge to our contentment, that this mindset will help us overcome. Although I think we would all say today that God's in charge, that God knows best, we tend to behave like this: "God knows everything, God is all wise, God knows best, but I think I'll handle my life. Sure, you need to handle those people's lives, but I've got a plan, and, Lord, here it is. If you would sign it, and make sure it happens, then I'll be content."

When we say like that, we know it's folly. It's folly because we don't know everything and because we can't even accomplish what is best. God knows. And if we will trust him, then we know that everything that comes into our lives, even though there may be evil behind it as it was for Joseph, still God will use these things for the good. You can't control the world. So, you might as well trust God to do it. And he will do it for the good of all those who know him, all those who love him, and all those who are called according to his purpose.

Well, this comes up several other places but let me move us to chapter 3 verse 7. Paul has just given us his pedigree. He's told us his accomplishments. This is his resume, which is at the top of the Jewish world at the time. He has all these important things, but we should know in the storyline of Paul's life, he's lost those things now. So, he says, "But whatever gain I had, whatever I had that would have gotten me comfort, consumption, and credit, that would put me on the top of the world, I counted as loss for the sake of Christ."

Now let me just hold there for a minute. There is a way of explaining Christianity that's well intended but it stops at that verse. This approach says something like this, "You want to serve Jesus? It's hard. You lose everything. That's the way it is, and you better be happy about it." Well, there's truth in that, and it does push against those who say, "Trust Jesus, and you'll get everything you want." That's a prosperity gospel, what I always call "the name it, claim it, call it, haul it, blab it, grab it" approach. That's not the true gospel, but neither is it right simply to leave the call at "You'll lose everything. Just do it anyway. It's good for you."

Paul says here, "Whatever gain I had, I counted as loss for the sake of Christ. Indeed, I count everything as loss *because* of the surpassing worth of knowing Christ Jesus, my Lord" (3:8). That's the point. It's not to say that nothing else is good. The whole thing is about being so enamored with Christ and recognizing what he's done that all these other things fade so that when we really know this, when it sinks down into our souls, we're not having to say, "Alright, Jesus is better," but we realize he is so amazing. That yes, I love to be healthy, but if I lose health, I gain Christ. He is far surprising. If I lose everything that I might have, he is so much more. And if we don't get that, nothing else is going to click. This is why it's so important for us to be students of the Scriptures. That's why we have classes that everybody takes with the Scriptures. Even in our own reading in the church, that's how we come to know who Christ is. There are all kind of voices coming at us all the time telling us, "Look here, find satisfaction there." None of those are going to help us recognize the amazingness of Jesus, but the Scriptures will do that (and your interaction with believers who know these truths).

This is a shorthand of the gospel, so let me just remind us what it says. The reason that Christ is so amazing to us is not just the abstract realities of who he is. Amazing as that is, the stress is on what he's done for us. Remember, we have all sinned against God. We've all fallen short of his glory, and because of that the whole, full, hot, furious wrath of God hangs over our heads. And we deserve it. A good God *must* pour that out upon us. And what that's going to look like is eternal torment. That is just and fair. It's what we deserve, and we can't change it. No matter what we do, no matter how hard we try, we can't undo that. We can't escape. We're stuck. And yet, God, being rich in mercy because of his great love with which he loved us, has sent his Son, the Lord Jesus, as we read just a moment ago, to come and to suffer in this life and to hang on a cross and to bear on himself all of that wrath for everybody who would believe so that people like you and me, if we will trust Jesus and find in him our all in all, then all of that punishment which we deserve is taken away. We couldn't rescue ourselves, and yet he's done it on our behalf. And if we know this glorious reality, that is why we say, "Jesus is more!" He has done this for us, and, therefore, we set our hope and our contentment in him.

Now, in my mind's eye, what I see in the world is the mass of humanity rushing toward what they think will bring contentment. And it's a cliff, and they're just streaming this way. And here is the Lord through his Word saying, "This is not it. Here is the way to contentment." But nobody's listening. They're just running off the cliff, wave after wave of humanity. And if we were sober minded for just a moment, we could stand here in our rush to the cliff and say, "Some of those people who just fell off the cliff, they seem to have everything I think is going to bring me contentment. They have wealth. They have power. They have prestige. They have popularity. But I can tell they're not satisfied." And yet the wave of humanity says, "Well, it'll be different for me." And people continue to choose that. But if we look at this wave of humanity, we find amongst that wave many, many professing believers. While we know that God says, "Contentment is in Christ," we say, "Yeah, but I'd like to hedge my bet. I'd like to go along with this a little bit too." And this text, this day, is saying to all of us, "Chasing contentment in all these other things, will only lead to ruin. But Christ is all in all."

If you will trust what he's done for you at the cross and rest in him, you can be satisfied. You can then know that, no matter what anybody else says, the Lord has made you his own and nobody can pry you out of his hand. You can be secure and satisfied. You can be content and, therefore calm. You can have this, but it is only in Christ. So, I do plead with you this morning. Some of you don't really know this Jesus. You know about him, but you've never trusted him. And all that you have right now hanging over your head is the wrath of God. But he pleads with you this morning. Turn to him. He tells us he takes no delight in the death of the wicked. But there is rejoicing in the presence of the angels for every sinner who repents. That's not the angels rejoicing. That's rejoicing in the presence of the angels. Who's in the presence of the angels? God himself. God himself would rejoice for you to repent and believe this day.

And, then, those of you who know him, we get pulled away by so many other things. I get pulled away by so many other things. It's been good for my soul to sit with this text awhile, to be reminded, "Set your heart on Christ. He is sufficient. He alone will satisfy." And then we can seek first the kingdom of God and his righteousness and know that all these things will be added unto us.

Chapter 8

THE BOOKENDS
OF THE LETTER

Philippians 4:21-23

Justin Wainscott[1]

Introduction

You can usually tell a lot about a book by the way it begins, can't you? Does it intrigue you? Does it grab your attention? Does it pique your interest? Does it give you enough to keep you reading? And often we're going to make up our minds whether or not we're going to read a book based solely on the way it begins, based on the first line or two.

I mean, who doesn't want to keep reading a book that begins with, "In a hole in the ground, there lived a hobbit"? You can't stop there; you've got to keep reading to find out what sort of creature a hobbit is and why it lives in a hole in the ground. Or think about Dickens' famous opening line in *A Tale of Two Cities*: "It was the best of times; it was the worst of times." You are drawn into the story by that one line.

But, of course, the way a book ends is important as well. You want all the loose ends tied up; you want all the mysteries solved; you want all your questions answered, all the conflict resolved. If a book begins well but doesn't end well, you feel like you've wasted your time. You want the ending to make sense of everything that was written from the beginning onward. You want the beginning and the ending to serve as bookends that tie together everything in between.

---

[13] Justin Wainscott is Associate Dean of University Ministries and the School of Theology and Missions at Union University, where he also serves as Assistant Professor of Ministry.

And friends, that's exactly what we have in this letter of Paul's to the Philippians. His opening greetings and his closing greetings serve as bookends to the whole letter. The opening greetings foreshadow themes that come up in the body of the letter, and the closing greetings offer reminders of those exact same themes. What he says at the beginning of the letter and again at the end of the letter makes sense of everything else in between, which means 1:1–2 and 4:21–23 are the bookends of this letter.

So, as we conclude this exposition of Philippians, I want us to hear these reminders that Paul offers to the church at Philippi and that the Holy Spirit offers anew to us. There are two themes that we're reminded of here in these closing verses: *unity* and *grace*. And though you may not remember it, these are the same two truths that are found in the opening verses of the letter as well. So, you can't really make sense of this letter without understanding the bookends of unity and grace. So, let's see them here in this closing text and consider how they help us make sense of the letter as a whole.

First, the reminder of unity.

1. Unity (4:21-22)

Now, we have to keep in mind that the biggest internal issue that the Philippian church faced was division. They were a church that was suffering discord and disharmony. And we have seen this issue hinted at and addressed in several places throughout the letter, but most emphatically in 4:2-3 where Paul writes: "I entreat Euodia and Syntyche to agree in the Lord. Yes, I ask you also, true companion, help these women . . ." This problem of disunity is what causes Paul to say what he says in places like 1:27 (". . . so that whether I come and see you or am absent, I may hear of you that you are standing firm in one spirit, with one mind striving side by side for the faith of the gospel . . .") and in 2:3-4 ("Do nothing from selfish ambition or conceit, but in humility count others more significant than yourselves. Let each of you look not only to your own interests, but also to the interests of others"). So, we know that division was something of a problem in this church, and we know that unity was needed.

So, look at the way Paul words his closing greetings in 4:21, "Greet every saint in Christ Jesus." Now, you may remember that in some of Paul's letters, he offers personal greetings to specific individuals as he draws the letter to a close. Greet Priscilla and Acquilla (Rom 16:3). Greet Andronicus and Junia (Rom 16:7). Greet those who belong to the family of Aristobulus (Rom 16:10). Greet Rufus (Rom 16:13). Give my greetings to Nympha and Archippus (Col 4:15, 17). But he doesn't do that here at the end of this letter. Why? Because he doesn't want to intensify any sort of envy or rivalry; he doesn't want to add to any of the division. Instead, he wants to foster unity, so he says, "Greet *every* saint in Christ Jesus."

And the key word there is *every*. Greet them all, every single one of them. Whether they sided with Euodia or Syntyche, it doesn't matter. I send every one of them my greetings, because they are all saints in Christ Jesus. That one word—every—reminds them of the unity that they share in Christ.

And remember, this is the same way he opened the letter. Look back at 1:1. "To *all* the saints in Christ Jesus who are at Philippi." Not to *some* of the saints or *most* of the saints, but to *all* of the saints in Christ Jesus. And then he continues to stress this unity throughout the letter. Look at the places this keeps coming up:

> "I thank my God in all my remembrance of you, always in every prayer of mine *for you all* . . ." (1:3-4).

> "It is right for me to feel this way *about you all*, because I hold you in my heart, for *you are all* partakers with me of grace . . ." (1:7).

"For God is my witness, how I yearn *for you all* with the affection of Christ Jesus" (1:9).

"Even if I am to be poured out as a drink offering upon the sacrificial offering of your faith, I am glad and rejoice *with you all*" (2:17).

And so, as he draws the letter to a close, he stresses this oneness, this unity, one last time when he says, "Greet *every* saint."

What Paul is stressing to these Philippian Christians, and what we should hear being stressed to us, is the reality of the unity we share with our brothers and sisters in the local church. We have seen this again and again in Philippians, and we need to be ever mindful of it. The blood of Jesus Christ has purchased our unity; he has made us one. But because of sin, our unity is always fragile. It must be handled with the utmost care and concern. So, let us strive to maintain the unity that Christ has so graciously granted to us. Let us constantly pray for and work for unity in our churches. Because, without unity, we will not be able to obey what we have read and learned in this letter.

But there is also a broader unity that is expressed here in these closing greetings. Because not only does Paul offer his personal greeting to every one of them, but the rest of verse 21 and the beginning of verse 22 provide greetings from the brothers who were with Paul and from all the saints in Rome, where Paul was imprisoned. "The brothers who are with me greet you. All the saints greet you, especially those of Caesar's household" (4:21-22). Thus, Paul was not just reminding them of the unity they shared with one another in that local church. He was also reminding them of the unity they shared with other saints in other places in the world, who were a part of other local churches. In other words, they shared a unity with the capital "C" Church as well. In Christ, they were not only united to every Christian in the church in Philippi, but they were also united to every Christian everywhere else. They were united to all the saints.

And brothers and sisters, so are we. Now, our denominational differences are significant and there are reasons they exist, but let's not ever lose sight of the fact that we are united to every saint in Christ Jesus, regardless of denomination or tradition. Whether they be Methodist or Presbyterian or Lutheran or Anglican or Pentecostal or anything in between, if they are truly in Christ, then they are fellow saints, brothers and sisters, co-heirs with Christ, members with us of the Church of the Lord Jesus Christ. And geography and ethnicity make no difference either. We have brothers and sisters all over the world who look nothing like us and sound nothing like us; but in Christ, we all belong to the same family. That's why you can go on an international mission trip and find that you have more in common with believers in a foreign country than you do with unbelievers in your own neighborhood. So, we need to recognize the unity that we share with all the saints in Christ. Paul is trying to establish that connection between these churches and between these brothers and sisters here, and we would do well to realize that those same kinds of connections still exist for us today.

So, unity is the first reminder that we see here. The second reminder that Paul offers to the Philippians and that the Spirit offers to us is a reminder of grace.

2. Grace (vv. 22-23)

Again, look at how grace bookends this letter. Look at 1:2, "*Grace to you* and peace from God our Father and the Lord Jesus Christ." And then look at 4:23, "*The grace of the Lord Jesus Christ* be with your spirit." Paul opens the letter with a blessing of divine grace, and now he closes it with a blessing of divine grace. He prays for the presence of grace to be with them. Now, I want you to realize that this is not just a really spiritual way to close a letter. This is not just some Christian way of saying, "Yours, sincerely." No, this closing line has great theological significance to everything that Paul has written since the opening line about God's grace. Because Paul knows, as we need to come to know, that left to ourselves, left to our strength and our own power and our own effort, we will not be able to live out the commands of this letter. We can't do it. Everything we are called to do in this letter is utterly impossible apart from the grace of Christ.

Without grace, our love will not abound more and more (1:9). Without grace, we will not approve what is excellent and so be pure and blameless for the day of Christ (1:10). Without grace, we will not be filled with the fruit of righteousness (1:11). Without grace, our manner of life will not be worthy of the gospel of Christ (1:27). Without grace, we will not stand firm in one spirit (1:27). Without grace, we will not withstand persecution with boldness and faith (1:28-30); we will not become bold to speak the word without fear (1:14). Without grace, we will not humbly consider others more significant than ourselves (2:3). Without grace, we will look only to our own interests, not the interests of others (2:4). Without grace, we will not work out our salvation with fear and trembling, trusting that God is at work in us, to will and to work for his good pleasure (2:12-13). Without grace, we will grumble and complain; we will not shine as lights in a darkened world, and we will not stand apart from this crooked and twisted generation (2:14-15). Without grace, we will not hold fast to the word of life (2:16). Without grace, we will not press on toward the goal of our heavenward call (3:14). Without grace, we will not follow the right examples, and our minds will become fixed on earthly things (4:8-9). Without grace, we will not resolve our conflicts with humility and love (4:2-3). Without grace, we will not rejoice in the Lord always (4:4); we will not be gentle to everyone (4:5); and we will not be prayerful about everything (4:6). Without grace, we will be anxious about everything, and we will not know the peace of God (4:6-7). Without grace, we will not be content in Christ (4:11-13). Without grace, we will not give sacrificially to help advance the gospel (4:14-16). Without grace, we will not trust that God will provide for our every need (4:19).

Nothing in this letter is attainable without the grace of the Lord Jesus Christ. Nothing we are called to here is possible without the grace of the Lord Jesus Christ. And that's why this letter begins and ends with grace.

So, if you think you can do this on your own, apart from divine grace, you are in for a rude awakening. If you think the Christian life is merely one of personal effort and achievement, then you are sadly mistaken. If you think you can keep these commands in and of your own strength, you do not understand the depths of our need for grace. We don't just need God's grace to *save* us; we need his grace to *sustain* us and *sanctify* us and *secure* us. Friends, saving grace is only one aspect of the grace of the Lord Jesus Christ. And thanks be to God for his saving grace—yes! But thanks be to God also for his sanctifying grace and his sustaining grace. Because without them, we would be saved from our sins, but we would still be left in our sins. Thankfully, God's grace not only saves us from our sins; it begins to sanctify us and lead us away from our sins toward holiness in Christ.

That's why we sing, "O to *grace*, how great a debtor, daily I'm constrained to be. Let Thy *grace*, Lord, like a fetter, bind my wandering heart to Thee. Prone to wander, Lord, I feel it; prone to leave the God I love. Here's my heart, Lord, take and seal it; seal it for Thy courts above." And that's why the last stanza of that hymn goes on to celebrate the glorifying, perfecting grace of God, which will finally and fully free us from our sins: "Oh that day, when free from sinning, I shall see Thy lovely face. Full-arrayed in blood-washed linen, how I'll sing Thy sovereign *grace*." We will sing and celebrate the fact that our salvation, from beginning to end—our justification, our sanctification, and our glorification—are all due to the grace of God. And that's why we need the grace of the Lord Jesus Christ to continue to be with us. Because without it, we cannot obey the commands of this letter; and without it, we will wander from the God we say we love.

Now, there's one last aspect of grace that I want us to see this morning. Not only are we reminded of our *need* for divine grace here at the end of this letter; we are also reminded of the *power* of divine grace. Not only does Paul pray for the grace of Christ to be with us; he illustrates its power here at the close of the letter. And this illustration of the power of divine grace would have been of enormous encouragement to the Philippians, and it should be to us as well.

Look again at verse 22: "All the saints greet you, *especially those of Caesar's household.*" This is the only specific group of people Paul mentions here in these closing greetings. Why mention them? What's the significance in mentioning "especially those of Caesar's household"? Because here was a vivid reminder that the power of Caesar was no match for the power of Christ. Oh, sure, Paul may have been suffering at the hands of Caesar; he may have been in Caesar's prison. And the Philippians themselves may have been suffering at the hands of Caesar's persecutions. Sure, Caesar may have been flexing his muscles, showing his imperial power; but here was a reminder that imperial power could not stop the power of the gospel. The grace of Christ had even infiltrated Caesar's household! There were members of Caesar's household, whether they were slaves or servants or soldiers, who had heard the gospel and believed and were now saints in Christ. There in the heart of the Roman Empire, another kingdom was rising. Knees were bowing, *not* before Caesar, but before Christ. Tongues were confessing not that "Caesar is Lord" but that "Jesus is Lord." Oh, what a beautiful reminder of the power of divine grace. And oh, what a motivation this should be for us to stand firm in the face of persecution, knowing that there is no power that rivals the power of God's grace.

Conclusion

And friends, just as we saw in chapter 3 that the grace of Christ turned Paul from a proud, self-righteous Pharisee to a humble, Christ-exalting apostle, so that same grace has been turning the hearts of people away from themselves and to Jesus Christ for over two thousand years now. And it can do the same for you today. No one is beyond the power of divine grace. God's grace can save you and sanctify you and sustain you and secure you. So, maybe today you need to receive the grace of God in Jesus Christ. You need to stop trusting in yourself and trying to earn God's favor and simply trust in Jesus Christ and what he has done for you by paying for your sins through his death on the cross and his resurrection from the dead. Believe in Jesus' death and resurrection; repent of your sins; and turn in faith to him to receive the saving grace of God today.

And maybe you are already a Christian, but you have been trying to live in obedience to God's Word in your own power and by your own effort alone. Or maybe you have become legalistic and self-righteous, forgetting that even your obedience is ultimately due to the working of God's grace. If either of those is true today, you need to give thanks for the grace of God that is continually at work within you, and you need to rest in that grace.

And then maybe you are a believer, but you have lost sight of just how amazing and how powerful God's grace really is. And you just need to repent of your hard-heartedness and cold-heartedness and celebrate the grace of God in Jesus Christ. You need to realize what a wonder it is that God saved a wretch like you, and you need to rejoice in the grace of God.

I want the word that Paul left ringing in the Philippians' ears to be what we leave with this morning ringing in our ears—grace. The grace of the Lord Jesus Christ be with your spirit.

UNION
UNIVERSITY

EXCELLENCE-DRIVEN
CHRIST-CENTERED
PEOPLE-FOCUSED
FUTURE-DIRECTED

UNION UNIVERSITY

Union University offers the following programs to
equip ministers and those training for ministry:

Undergraduate
www.uu.edu/programs/stm/academics/undergraduate

Graduate
www.uu.edu/programs/stm/academics/graduate

Memphis College of Urban and Theological Studies (MCUTS)
www.uu.edu/mcuts

Adult Studies
www.uu.edu/programs/soaps/academics/bachelor-christian-leadership

Ryan Center Bible Conference
www.uu.edu/centers/biblical/bible-conference

Dockery Lectures on Baptist Thought and Heritage
www.uu.edu/events/dockerylectures

W. D. Powell Missions Lectures
www.uu.edu/events/stmlectures

Equip Youth Apologetics Conference
www.uu.edu/events/equip

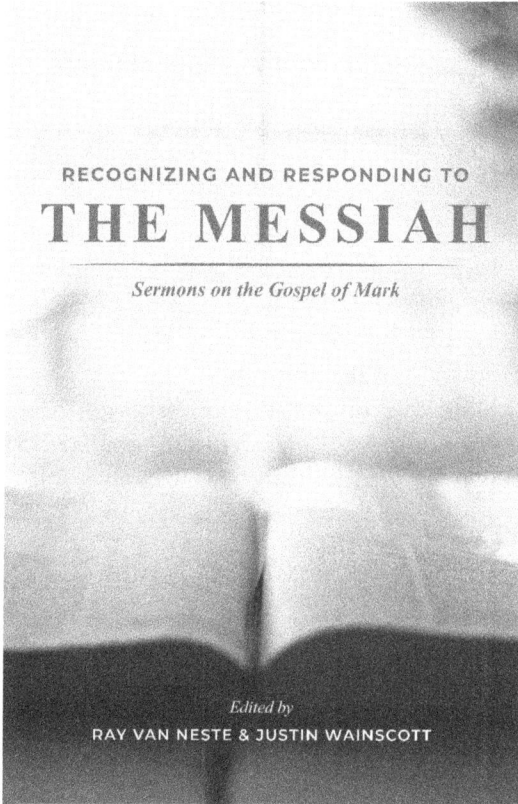

RECOGNIZING AND RESPONDING TO

THE MESSIAH

Sermons on the Gospel of Mark

Edited by
RAY VAN NESTE & JUSTIN WAINSCOTT

ALSO FROM

UNION UNIVERSITY | PRESS

Union University History
- James Alex Baggett, *So Great a Cloud of Witnesses: Union University, 1823-2000*
- Ray Van Neste & Justin Wainscott, eds., *Lest We Forget: Founders' Day Addresses from Union University - Bicentennial Edition*

Word Series (From sermon series preached in Union's Chapel)
- Ray Van Neste & Justin Wainscott, eds., *Recognizing and Responding to the Messiah: Sermons on the Gospel of Mark*

Religio et Eruditio (Best Senior Theses)
- Ray Van Neste & Jacob Shatzer, eds., *Volume 1: 2014-2015*
- Ray Van Neste & Jacob Shatzer, eds., *Volume 2: 2016-2017*
- Ray Van Neste & Jacob Shatzer, eds., *Volume 3: 2018-2019*
- Ray Van Neste & Jacob Shatzer, eds., *Volume 4: 2020-2022*

Future Scholars (Winning essays from our annual Bible and theology essay contest for high school juniors and seniors)
- Ray Van Neste & Jacob Shatzer, eds., *Volume 1: 2018*
- Ray Van Neste & Jacob Shatzer, eds., *Volume 2: 2019*
- Ray Van Neste & Jacob Shatzer, eds., *Volume 3: 2020*
- Ray Van Neste & Jacob Shatzer, eds., *Volume 4: 2021*
- Ray Van Neste & Justin Wainscott, eds., *Volume 5: 2023*

Forthcoming Book
- New edition of *The New Testament in the Language of the People* by Charles B. Williams, originally published in 1937 when Dr. Williams was a professor at Union.

UNION
UNIVERSITY
RELIGIO ET ERUDITIO

The *Heart of the Campus Campaign* is a key initiative to raise funds for a new chapel at the heart of Union University's campus, providing a space for worship, community, and spiritual growth. Your support will help shape the spiritual lives of students for generations. Join us in creating a space where faith and learning come together at the heart of Union University.

uu.edu/new/chapel

JOIN THE FACULTY WHO GAVE FIRST

GIVE TODAY!

In 2018, Union's School of **Theology and Missions** faculty gave the **first $10,000** to start an endowed scholarship for students pursuing God's call. That seed has grown by **over 500 percent**, now helping even more students called to ministry and theological study.

Help us support the next generation of gospel-centered leaders. **Support the STM Endowed Scholarship Fund.**

UNION UNIVERSITY
School of Theology and Missions

www.ingramcontent.com/pod-product-compliance
Lightning Source LLC
Chambersburg PA
CBHW060334050426
42449CB00011B/2752